Mentoring for School Quality

Other Books by the Authors

Mentoring with Meaning: How Educators Can Be More Professional and Effective

Mentoring for School Quality

How Educators Can Be More Professional and Effective

Edited by
Bruce S. Cooper and Carlos R. McCray

ROWMAN & LITTLEFIELD
Lanham • Boulder • New York • London

Published by Rowman & Littlefield
A wholly owned subsidiary of The Rowman & Littlefield Publishing Group, Inc.
4501 Forbes Boulevard, Suite 200, Lanham, Maryland 20706
www.rowman.com

Unit A, Whitacre Mews, 26-34 Stannary Street, London SE11 4AB, United Kingdom

British Library Cataloguing in Publication Information Available

Library of Congress Cataloging-in-Publication Data

McCray, Carlos R.
Mentoring for school quality : how educators can be more professional and effective / Carlos R. McCray and Bruce S. Cooper.
   pages cm
Includes bibliographical references and index.
ISBN 978-1-4758-1799-7 (cloth : alk. paper) — ISBN 978-1-4758-1800-0
(pbk. : alk. paper) — ISBN 978-1-4758-1801-7 (electronic) 1. Mentors in education.
2. Teachers—Training of. 3. Educational leadership. I. Cooper, Bruce S. II. Title.
LB1731.4.M44 2015
371.102—dc23
                                                              2015024403

Printed in the United States of America

Contents

Chapter 1

Building a Professional Relationship

Bruce S. Cooper

Mentoring can assist educators—including teachers, principals, guidance counselors, and other school staff—to think, act, and actually be more "professional." The term *mentoring* has important meanings as explored and applied in this book. "Mentoring with meaning" implies that adults teaching children should and can embody the meanings and actions of true, active professionalism. And becoming a good teacher requires both that neophytes be open to learning and that senior staff and leaders be willing to be exemplary, adaptive, and "helpful to other teachers to be outstanding teachers."

This chapter begins with a historical (but not hysterical) view of *professionalism in education*, that along with other traditional "female jobs" (such as social work, nursing, *and* teaching) have long been deemed "semiprofessional." As such, teachers are not considered a true "profession," such as medical doctors and lawyers, whose activities often have importance in real life (and death) situations. Men make money while women just work hard, as the saying goes.

One male teacher experienced the following when trying to raise a family on a teacher's salary:

Richie Brown, a North Carolina educator who was a candidate for teacher of the year, is the type of teacher whom every principal should want. He was teaching in a high-demand subject area in a low-income school just outside of Wilmington, North Carolina. However, Brown decided to *leave the profession* last year after six years of teaching, and the reason was simple: he did not earn enough money to support his family. (Boser & Straus, 2014, p. 4)

In the 1960s, working with his mentor, Amitai Etzioni (1969), on a book, *The Semi-Professions and Their Organization*, Daniel C. Lortie contributed the "teachers'" analysis chapters, showing what was lacking for teachers in their work that prevented them from being real professionals. Later, Lortie (1975) published his own now-classic book in the field, *Schoolteacher: A Sociological Study*, which spells out the qualities of teaching and how the skills are understood, taught, and practiced by teachers, and whether they are seen as "professionals" or just "semiprofessionals."

Or as a review of Lortie's book explains:

Upon its initial publication, many reviewers dubbed Dan C. Lortie's *School-teacher* (1975) the best social portrait of the profession since Willard W. Waller's classic, *The Sociology of Teaching* (1932). This new printing of Lortie's classic—including a new preface bringing the author's observations up to date—is an essential view into the world and culture of a vitally important profession.

These missing professional qualities included the following: (1) absence of real, in-depth quality training; (2) lack of key skills and practices; (3) responsibilities that keep teachers and teaching from true professional standing; and (4) the need for schools to be able to use true measures of teacher effectiveness.

Lortie (1969) also characterized teaching as an "art" (like acting), and not really a profession at all. He explained:

Continual claims to "professional" status presume the existence of a unified occupational group with a system of collegial help and controls. The rhetoric of "teaching as an art," however, projects autonomy rather than control; to use the artist as a prototype is to stress individuality rather than standardization through bureaucratic or collegial controls. (1969, p. 1)

This having been said, teachers and their mentors still play a critical role in schools—and have an important relationship to society. Teachers are essential in educating and socializing the next generation of children, including kids aged from about three or four to nineteen years old in preschool through high school (PreK through twelfth grade). Teachers, even if they lack the skills to control students' behaviors and lives, can and do still have a strong and important influence on their pupils.

These forces and influences include seeing that students are well prepared for tests, for promotion through the grade levels, and graduation—leading to more further and higher education—and eventually employment, a decent income, and full participation in adult life. As Cooper and Mulvey (2012) explained: "Society must promote a quality education, available health services, and financial equity and opportunity for all" (p. 22).

Professionalism, as critical to mentoring, has five distinct, important qualities that form the basis of this chapter, as follows:

1. We connect the two ideas, thus explaining what mentoring and semiprofessionalism share in meaning and applications.
2. We then discuss why teaching is often considered "semiprofessional" and the implications for mentoring others in crucial methods and processes.
3. We also give examples of how teachers are, can be, and should be "mentored" by others in fields of pedagogy, psychology, and sociology.
4. We discuss how electronic equipment and other technologies can likely help raise the standards for education, improving teacher-to-teacher interactions and student test results, and thus the overall enterprise in the future.
5. We then prescribe a coordinated system for helping teachers succeed during all phases of their careers, from starting out as new "practice teachers" through veteran life in the classroom, school, district, and community.

TECHNOLOGY

In some ways, teaching has become more effective, some believe, because like other professional activities, classroom instruction has been made better and stronger by the increased use of technology in the pedagogy of teachers and the learning of students. As one observer stated:

> The most compelling constants in teaching around the world revolve around communication and connections between students and cultures. The advent of new ways to communicate and interact over the last century—and, in a way relevant to education, within the last fifty years—has dramatically changed the face of the profession. The photographs, telephones, slide shows, filmstrips, videotapes, Internet, and video-conferencing that exist in schools today show a steady (not slow) adoption of technology within instruction. (https://www.msu.edu/~tuckeys1/ education/courses/te902_paper.pdf)

Dan Lortie makes several arguments based on sociological research on teachers in his classic book *Schoolteacher*, but only a few beliefs are essential, in particular.

Lortie furthered this view by using data in Chapter 2 to support the notion that teachers are, at the very least, culpable. Second, many of his arguments and conclusions, although perhaps relevant and valid in the mid-1960s, are suspect in our twenty-first-century educational atmosphere.

In his historical walk-through of schooling in Chapter 1, Lortie discusses the *slowness* of change in the field in an unusual way—by comparing it to the endeavor of agriculture. He claims that "the principal modes of instruction (e.g., lecturing, recitation, demonstration, seat work, small-group instruction, etc.) were known and used years ago" (p. 23), thus implying that the wide range of newer methods are being ignored.

Furthermore, by comparing teachers—who are ignoring newer methods in their classrooms—with farmers employing more advanced methods in their *fields* (pun intended) and receiving greater yields in productivity to boot, it is obvious to Lortie that teachers are just not advancing fast enough. I fundamentally disagree with this argument on several levels.

First, Lortie makes a direct comparison between a physical activity involving an individual's actions toward the goal of improved crop cultivation and the (mostly) intellectual-psychological and social activity in which an individual's actions can affect the goals of cultivating mental capacity and learning for students. These educational concepts are infinitely more subtle and complex than the scientific control of the growth of plants and animals. Both may happen naturally (even without a farm or a school), but dealing with classrooms full of children with their human minds, emotion, psyches, needs, and motivations are not something to be easily categorized and compared with food production.

Second, the assertion that technical advances in agriculture are equivalent to "advances" in schooling is suspect. Lortie states that teachers do not claim to teach more in less time as if this were a drawback. Equivalently, one could claim that sculptors are "nonproductive" if they do not produce more statues in less time and playwrights are simply not pumping out enough plays per annum. Teachers, although perhaps not falling into the same artisan category as these examples mentioned, are engaged in a truly human endeavor. These human aspects make the outcomes subject to complex changing demands and expectations.

Given the limited funding due to school budgets being derived primarily from a politicized tax base and low amounts of user support for changing technologies, it is astounding that schoolteachers have managed to incorporate these technological advancements into their "principal modes of instruction" that Lortie so readily dismisses as dated—back in the pre-tech age of chalkboards, handouts, and roll-down maps.

This raises another issue with *Schoolteacher*. Surely, Lortie cannot be faulted for neglecting to discuss the relevance of *information technology* in the way teachers work. This book, nearing its third decade in circulation, tells an interesting story about the development and present circumstances of teachers, but only up to the middle of the last century. Are situations involving women in teaching still statistically as skewed as they were at the time of his survey analysis, or has the face of the profession changed drastically?

COMPLEXITY OF ENTRY INTO THE PROFESSIONS

Another quality of professional preparation revolves around the effort and time necessary to gain admission and certification into a profession.

For doctors, the years needed to learn and master medical skills are quite numerous and expensive, and continue as physicians may specialize and train, for example, as surgeons, endocrinologists, or urologists. Exams are given along the way, as doctors are tested on their knowledge and skills in their fields. Professionalism, by its very nature, implies that one group of doctors, for example, both train and test the neophytes as their mentors to make sure the trainees (or mentees) are knowledgeable and skilled in their specialty so as not to embarrass their colleagues and disgrace their profession (not to mention hurting, disabling, or killing their clients).

Thus, while teaching is less critical or life endangering than results of the law and medicine, we know that in many ways children who receive poor, inadequate, or hurtful education may be "disabled" throughout their adult lives and thus be on welfare, physically unwell, and nonproductive in their jobs and profession.

ELECTIVE VERSUS SELECTIVE ADMISSIONS

To what extent are graduate schools for teaching highly selective in admissions, testing, and preparation? To qualify as a professional, many analysts feel that it may be too easy "to become" a teacher, both gaining entry and getting to stay on and obtain "tenure" if offered and available. Rarely does one hear about teachers being thrown out or denied admission to the role. And once tenure is awarded, the job may go on for a lifetime.

TEACHER BASHING IS FUN BUT COSTLY

Attacking teachers is often easy, but seeing teachers defending themselves often is not. In seeing this in *Rethinking Schools* (2010),

> Teachers can defend themselves from this hailstorm of criticism only if they make common cause with everyone who has a stake in defending—and transforming—public schools. In this struggle, teachers and parents need each other. But building successful coalitions and strategies takes hard work. Many parents, particularly parents of color, are angry and frustrated by long-term dysfunctions in schools that make it difficult for their children to learn and succeed. . . . Teachers too often see the families and communities from which their students come as obstacles to overcome. But successful teaching and successful organizing are based on recognizing the strengths inherent in families and communities. (pp. 4–5)

Other research has investigated the effects of professional staff development on the lives and jobs of teachers in the United States. As one study (Van den Bergh, Ros, & Beijaard, 2014) found:

Results show that several aspects of feedback during active learning were improved, both in the short and in the long term. It is concluded that the professional development of teachers can be effective and sustainable, if certain conditions are met. (p. 33)

GENDER OF THE PROFESSIONS

Another quality of teaching—along with nursing and social work—is that women have dominated these fields. Etzioni points out in the preface to his book *The Semi-Professions and Their Organization* (1969) that "the typical professional is a male where the typical semi-professional is a female" (p. xv). (This ratio is changing, as law, medical, and business—and even veterinary—schools have more female students now than males attending them in many cases.)

COORDINATION AND TEAMWORK

Another limitation of being a teacher is the absence of teamwork and a shared sense of mission and identity. As Smilansky (1984) found, not surprisingly, that having good and positive feelings in teachers' work was divided. Positive feelings about their jobs for teachers related mostly to *work in the classroom*, while personal anxiety and stress were typically triggered by "external factors" such as working with supervisors (e.g., principals and assistant principals/department chairs) and being judged by ever-critical societies and school systems.

Smilansky (1984) noted that:

> Teachers' general satisfaction and stress at work were found to relate mostly to their reported feelings about what happened within the class rather than to administrative or policy factors (e.g., satisfaction in life in general and personal feelings of self-efficacy), while reported stress was related to *external factors* (e.g., principal and pupil ratings). The "better" teachers, according to external rating, were willing to report more stress in their work situation. (p. 88)

Thus, teaching is a lonely, somewhat isolated and isolating job, with only limited opportunities to do the following: (1) share good ideas, methods, and practices; (2) ventilate about job stress; and (3) learn and share effective methods and materials. And with greater use of "electronic" instruction and learning, students can spend hours staring at a computer screen. Thus, schools are leaving and closing most of the interactive, group activities to student participation in clubs, music groups, and of course, sports and school clubs.

MENTORING TEACHERS AS PROFESSIONALS

Key to mentoring is the working relationship between the mentor and the mentee, the veteran and the newcomer. As such, most professions require a term/year or two of mentoring and interning for certification and mutual help, where the newcomers learn the job, the skills, attitudes, and methods—even the "tricks of the trade"—from the old-timers, and are evaluated on their performance before becoming a member of the profession.

It's a two-way street, where mentors are willing and able to help and teach the newer members of the education professions and the younger colleagues are willing and able to learn and reflect best practices from the expert old-timers and "be mentored." And education needs to establish and build these relationships between the more expert (the "mentor") and the less knowledgeable (called "mentees"), if schools are to improve.

In this chapter, we explain mentoring—that is, the process—and how it is often done successfully between neophytes and their senior colleagues who know the field and have successful records as teachers, school leaders, or other professionals.

We introduce the importance of the mentoring process, and what the book will cover and show. Mentoring is a complex, personal, and interpersonal process that has long been around but not always done and understood in schools. In fact, teachers work alone, for the most part, and find it difficult to locate and follow a mentor. Hence, how can teaching become a more collective, active, and innovative process if teachers don't work together and mentor one another?

This chapter presents and analyzes the steps and stages of mentoring, including the following activities:

1. how best to define and activate mentoring in schools, and what can often inhibits the process
2. what can be done to boost mentoring in education, including schools and classrooms
3. what prevents and inhibits mentoring in some education systems and school settings
4. give some remarkable examples of mentoring that can inform other school and classroom settings and can thus support the process.

KEY QUALITIES OF THE PROFESSIONS

Three C's (collegiality, community, and commitment), and *three P's* (prestige, pride, and productivity) are all essential to mark and promote professionalism for teachers and administrators and for schools of education to help teachers to make a more successful and long-lasting entry into the field.

The three *C*'s are vital to all professions—and all groups seeking such status. Below are a brief description and analysis of these qualities.

The first *C*, *collegiality*, is important from the onset to help teachers gain respect working together and to support each other, from the first days in their teaching positions. "Student teachers" or "practice teachers" enter a new school environment, hoping (praying) and expecting that the regular teaching and administrative staff will and does welcome and care about them. Most teachers remember those first few days on the job for the rest of their careers, and how they earnestly wanted to feel and sought a *community* of colleagues to assist and help them to share a collective sense of purpose; that is, people to support and help them in creating the sense of shared *community* (the second *C*) in the job and school.

Lortie noted almost fifty years ago the tensions for teachers, between all being treated alike and having discretion as real individuals and professionals. As others have explained the issue:

> Teaching is a complex endeavor. Combined factors, such as student motivation and the instructor's rapport with the students, have the potential to influence how effective any technique is. Thus, any data taken from a classroom are inherently contaminated and may not provide a perfect picture of effectiveness. . . .

While results indicated that lecturing was the least effective technique, it should be noted that students still scored relatively high after lecturing alone, which indicates that learning was still occurring. . . . In the end, instructors must decide for themselves, and be confident in their decisions, regarding what techniques to use, what material to use it with, and how often to use them. (Tomcho & Foels, 2008, p. 288–89).

That is probably the real underlying solution to the effectiveness of any teaching technique (Hackathorn et al., 2011, p. 51).

The professions require a high level of *commitment* (the third *C*) and dedication, as working to help cohorts of students over 183 days per year is a long-term commitment—and somehow teachers are expected to show progress with students over two-thirds of a year's period that may be increasing in length. In fact, few other professions involve such long-term (continuous) personal servicing, with daily face-to-face interactions, as teacher work to nurture and support students week in and week out.

Despite all this time spent teaching, these educators devote amazingly little time and effort to mentoring one another, teacher to teacher, while in the classroom. Instead, teaching is perhaps one of the "loneliest of professions," where, for example, a recent colleague had been a tenth-grade math teacher for forty-eight years and when she retired, she closed her door and left her school, alone. She had lived through a long, lonely career in teaching.

Rarely if ever did she advocate, or was she able to share lessons and techniques with her fellow teachers and colleagues. Little time was available and allocated for teachers to meet and share new ideas, methods, curriculum, or strategies with colleagues. It was every woman and man for herself or himself. Even now in the age of electronic communications, teachers rarely "broadcast"—or exchange—new ideas, pedagogy, or curriculum with other colleagues, declaring: "Look what worked in my class today! Would you like me to help you do it in yours?"

Or, in her study of the "semiprofession" of social work, like teaching, Homans (1962) found, "If one of the parties has authority over the other, the more frequently one of the two originates interaction for the other, the stronger will be the latter's sentiment of respect (or hostility) toward her, and the more nearly will the frequency of interactions be kept to the amount typical of the whole system" (p. 247). And things have not changed much—for teachers, social workers, and other semiprofessionals who are neither very interactive nor often treated like lawyers or doctors.

When compared to physicians, nurses realized that hospitals must change the way nurses are treated if they are to grow professionally, and teachers are much the same in the way their bosses (superintendents and principals) treat them. Fred E. Katz (1969) makes nursing (unlike teaching) to be more professional, concluding that

the new professional aspirations, however, with their focus on the nurse as a *scientific colleague* of physicians, hold the promise of making personalized care of patients increasingly sophisticated. But hospitals [like schools] will have to develop adequate arrangement for translating the new sophistication of nurses into workable organizational patterns. (p. 76)

The *three P's* (prestige, pride, and productivity) can be seen as part of the results of both mentoring and being mentored, doing professional work, and having productive lives. The first P, *prestige*, is certainly less obvious for teachers and other educators compared to doctors, lawyers, engineers, and many other professionals. In part, this reduced sense of prestige was associated with the large numbers of women in schools as teachers and administrators.

And *pride* that follows is the second P, as teachers and their colleagues show pride in their work but are often not recognized and praised for their contributions.

And finally, the third P, *productivity*, is often difficult for teachers to demonstrate (prove) and improve, although attempts to use student "growth" indicators and other "value-added models" (VAMs) have begun to reward those teachers who can demonstrate the growth and improvement of their students on tests, attendance, and achievement. VAM, for example, is defined as:

a method of teacher evaluation that measures the teacher's contribution in a given year by comparing the current test scores of their students to the scores of those same students in previous school years, as well as to the scores of other students in the same grade. In this manner, value-added modeling (VAM) seeks to isolate the contribution, or value added, that each teacher provides in a given year, which can be compared to the performance measures of other teachers. (McCaffrey et al., 2003, p. 1)

Critics say that the use of tests to evaluate individual teachers has not been scientifically validated, and many of the students' results are due to chance or conditions beyond the teacher's control, such as outside tutoring. Research shows, however, that differences in teacher effectiveness, as measured by the value added of teachers, are associated with very large economic effects on students (Cooper & Mulvey, 2012).

COMPENSATION FOR TEACHERS—BY WHAT STANDARD?

Another quality of teaching that may keep it from being a true profession is the way teachers are compensated, and around what standards. Since teachers are highly unionized and are using collective bargaining now to set pay and benefits, it is difficult to adjust and set individual "pay-to-performance" standards and practices. Lortie (1969) noted these facts years ago when he wrote:

Salaries are *set automatically* when the amount of compensation is beyond the power of administrators to determine. Promotion is also a relatively weak sanction as many teachers are not interested in leaving the classroom for an administrative position. And dismissal is used almost exclusively with beginning teachers, as tenure arrangements make it extremely difficult for school boards to discharge teachers on a continuing contract. (emphasis added; p. 8)

And since teachers' unions (e.g., the National Education Association and American Federation of Teachers, AFL-CIO) have grown and become more powerful, salaries are now usually set by two fixed criteria after collective negotiations are done, with neither having much to do with individual teachers' competencies or accomplishments. These are: (1) *years of teaching experience* as a teacher, and (2) professional or academic *degrees and graduate credits* earned—and not usually performance in the classrooms and schools, which are more difficult to measure for 3.7 million schoolteachers in the United States.

MAKING MENTORING WORK FOR
TEACHERS AND SUPERVISORS

Thus, how can other colleagues and their supervisors—the principals, assistant principals, and academic department chairs—mentor teachers? And how can these mentoring models (MMs) be created, taught, and made positive examples among teachers in their schools? Associations of educators believe that these goals are both practical and ethical, and relate to daily practices for every teacher in every classroom.

We see answers or foci to be moving in the right direction, based on the meanings of "mentoring" in education and other "professions." One immediate difference between mentoring in education and, say, medicine or law, are the lack of stature and authority of teachers compared to other groups. Thus, doctors as a group mentor themselves and their colleagues (often through the American Medical Association), as do lawyers and their legal organizations (e.g., American Bar Association).

ETHICS OF EDUCATION

The distinguished American Association of Educators (AAE) Advisory Board and the executive committee of the Association developed the Code of Ethics for Educators. The code contains three main principles relating to the rights of students and educators.

1. The professional educator strives to create a learning environment that nurtures their clients—the students—to fulfill the potential of all children in their classes.
2. The professional educator acts with a conscientious effort to exemplify the highest ethical standards.
3. The professional educator responsibly accepts that every child has a right to an uninterrupted education, free from strikes or any other union work stoppage tactics.

All this having been said, we know now that teaching, like other professions, is based on these principles that contribute to it being a "profession"— thus requiring professional behavior. And mentors should keep in mind these following principles, demonstrating, reinforcing, and strengthening these ethical beliefs in their schools and classrooms:

PRINCIPLE I: Ethical Conduct toward Students
We know that "professionalism" in education begins with instructing and helping children (pupils) based on these four principles. The professional

educator, in accepting his or her position of public trust, measures success not only by the progress of each student toward the realization of his or her personal potential but also as a citizen of the greater community of the republic, listed below:

1. The professional educator deals considerately and justly with each student, and seeks to resolve problems, including disciplinary, legal, and political.
2. The professional educator does not intentionally expose the students to disparagement.
3. The professional educator does not reveal confidential information or results concerning students, unless required by law.
4. The professional educator makes a concerted effort to protect students from conditions detrimental to learning, health, or safety.

PRINCIPLE II: Ethical Conduct toward Clients and their Performance
The professional educator assumes responsibility and accountability for his or her performance and continually strives to demonstrate competence, based on these principles:

1. The professional educator applies for, accepts, or assigns a position or a responsibility on the basis of professional qualifications, and adheres to the terms of a contract or appointment.
2. The professional educator maintains sound mental health, physical stamina, and social prudence necessary to perform the duties of any professional assignment.
3. The professional educator continues professional growth.
4. The professional educator complies with written local school policies and applicable laws and regulations that are not in conflict with this code of ethics.
5. The professional educator does not intentionally misrepresent official policies of the school or educational organizations, and clearly distinguishes those views from personal opinions.

PRINCIPLE III: Ethical Conduct toward Professional Colleagues
The professional educator, in exemplifying ethical relations with colleagues, provides just and equitable treatment to all members of the profession by complying with the following:

1. The professional educator does not reveal confidential information concerning colleagues unless required by law.
2. The professional educator does not willfully make false statements about a colleague or the school system.

3. The professional educator does not interfere with a colleague's freedom of choice, and works to eliminate coercion that forces educators to support actions and ideologies that violate individual professional integrity.

PRINCIPLE IV: Ethical Conduct toward Parents and Community
The professional educator pledges to protect public sovereignty over public education and private control of private education. These educators recognize that quality education is the common goal of the public—particularly boards of education and educators—and that a cooperative effort is essential among these groups to attain that goal. These activities include the following three actions:

1. The professional educator makes concerted efforts to communicate to parents all information that should be revealed in the interest of the student.
2. The professional educator endeavors to understand and respect the values and traditions of the diverse cultures represented in the community and in his or her classroom.
3. The professional educator manifests a positive and active role in school/community relations.

Also from an international perspective, teachers and their organizations can and do play critical roles in helping children and their families to get a good education—for their future—and to fight against social ills, such as "child labor." As the International Labour Organization explained (http://www.ilo.org/ipec/Partners/Teachers/Teacherseducatorsandtheirorganization-sasagentsofsocialchange/lang--en/index.htm):

It is vital that teachers and their organizations participate in decision-making and in educational planning and reform. The very nature of teachers' organizations as advocates for teachers' rights makes them effective partners in realizing and maximizing the potential of education in the fight against child labour. All the analyses on the relation between education and child labour point to the urgent need to improve the status of teachers and their working conditions and to address their continuing development as professionals. These are prerequisites for improving the quality of education in all countries, especially in developing countries where most of the world's child labourers live.

REFERENCES

Boser, U., & Straus, C. (2014). Mid- and late-career teachers struggle with paltry incomes. *Center for American Progress.*
Cooper, B. S., & Mulvey, J. D. (2012). *Intersections of children's health, education, and welfare.* New York: Palgrave-Macmillan Press.

Cooper, B. S., & Sureau, J. (2008). The collective politics of teacher unionism. In *Handbook of education politics and policy*, First Edition. Edited by B. S. Cooper, J. G. Cibulka, & L. D. Fusarelli, 263–310. New York: Routledge/Taylor & Francis.

Etzioni, A. (ed.) (1969). *The semi-professions and their organization.* New York: Macmillan.

Hackathorn, J., et al. (2011). Learning by doing: An empirical study of active teaching techniques. *Journal of Effective Teaching 11* (2), 40–54.

Homans, G. H. (1962). *The human group.* London: Routledge & Kegan Paul.

Katz, F. E. (1969). Nurses. In *The semi-professions and their organization.* Edited by A. Etzioni, 54–81. New York: The Free Press/Macmillan Company.

Lortie, D. C. (1969). The balance of control and autonomy in elementary school teaching (chapter 1). In *The semi-professions and their organization.* Edited by A. Etzioni, 1–53. New York: Macmillan.

Lortie, D. C. (1975). *Schoolteacher: A sociological study.* Chicago: University of Chicago Press.

McCaffrey, D. F., Lockwood, J. R., Koretz, D. M., & Hamilton, L. S. F. (2003). *Evaluating value-added models for teacher accountability.* New York: Carnegie Corporation, Rand.

Rethinking Schools Editorial. Teacher layoffs and war. http://www.rethinking-schools.org/archive/25_01/edit251.shtml

Smilansky, J. (1984). External and internal correlates of teachers' satisfaction and a willingness to report stress. *British Journal of Education Psychology 54* (1), 84–92.

Tomcho, T. J., & Foels, R. (2008). Assessing effective teaching of psychology: A meta-analytic integration of learning outcomes. *Teaching of Psychology 35*, 286–96.

Van den Bergh, L., Ros, A., & Beijaard, D. (2014). Feedback during active learning: Elementary school teachers' beliefs and perceived problems. *Educational Studies 39* (4), 418–30.

Waller, W. W. (1932). *The sociology of teaching.* New York: Wiley.

Chapter 2

Mentoring for School Improvement

Laverne C. Nimmons

INTRODUCTION

How can a school create a positive learning culture, raise expectations, increase student achievement, improve instructional practices, and build capacity in an impoverished urban community? This chapter explains how one school used mentoring to turn itself around, from a failing school to a National Blue Ribbon School of Excellence. Not only was this acknowledged as a top school in the district, but also it was nationally recognized as a top performing school.

One can only imagine that it takes a great deal of commitment, trust, and skill. The Cooper Elementary School, located in Central Brooklyn in the seventh poorest community in New York, has surpassed all expectations of student achievement, changing the school culture, and unifying around a common goal assuring that every child succeeds. Through transformational leadership that involved the mentoring of administrators, teachers, students, and parents, the principal has turned the school around from a failing school to a successful one.

Cheliotes and Reilly (2010) write about the idea of a leader-mentor in their book, *Coaching Conversations*. As a principal of a low-performing school that she turned around and made into a Blue Ribbon School, she states that the work of mentoring for school improvement takes a skilled leader who:

> asks questions, listens to the content and underlying themes in the answers, and then is able to integrate the group's thinking into a vision and direction to which people respond. This kind of leadership taps into the thinking and passions of others by seeking to develop the strengths and interests of others. It is not one person that determines success; it is the group that creates success. This engenders a culture of continuous improvement for all and shared pride in achievements. (p. 12)

The team organized efforts with clearly defined expectations, goals, and strategies that were used to create a community in which excellence was the only option. A clear and strong understanding of the responsibilities of the stakeholders—and the roles they played as team members—was demonstrated and markedly established the delivery and focus of accountability.

Cheliotes and Reilly (2010) describe mentoring leadership as

a "softer" form of directing. The thinking is that if I teach others what I know, they will handle situations as well as I do. At its best, it teaches necessary skills and insights to people who are new to their roles or positions. The mentor-leader spends time teaching others and offering options. Mentors often use the tools of storytelling and advising. They tell stories about what worked when they had that problem or issue. They advise others about best actions to take in a given situation. The mentor takes on the role of a *"wise one"* who guides another person to know what to do, based on the mentor's own thinking and experiences. (p. 13)

In developing the school, stakeholders questioned themselves about its fundamental purpose, and asked, "What does a high-performing school look like when it is structured around a commitment of academic excellence for all?" The answers to this question held many meaningful outcomes. In this case, achievement was not a singular goal for students; it is a goal for everyone. All educators were committed to great success for all students. The idea of "whatever it takes" to achieve academic excellence became the school's refrain. Rutherford (2005) states:

In such a school student success is a criterion for measuring the success of teachers collectively and individually. It is the norm for all to examine student work and use what is learned to make decisions about instruction. In such a school teacher and administrative success is the criteria for measuring the success of everyone else. That is, it is the collective goal of staff to have a fully qualified and satisfied teacher in each classroom so that more students can be successful more of the time. In such a school general education teachers, special education teachers, and administrators study and learn together. In such a school value is placed on shared leadership, responsibility, and decision-making in recognition of individual and collective commitment to student learning. (p. 3)

The Cooper School is a fifty-four-year-old building serving four hundred general education students, eighteen English language learners (ELLs), and forty-five special needs students in grades prekindergarten through five. The majority of students live within the boundaries of the community school district. The school shares the building with Cooper Middle School and is an essential part of the community for many of the students and their families.

The student body consists of 87 percent African American, 12 percent Hispanic, and 1 percent other, with a proportion of 90 percent Title I poor students. The children are served by professionals and support staff members, including the following: principal, assistant principal, individualized educational planning teacher, general education guidance counselors, special needs guidance counselor, general education teachers, teachers of special needs students, teacher specialists (cluster teachers), special education teacher support services (SETSS) for special needs children, adaptive physical education teacher, speech teacher, ELL teacher, and paraprofessionals.

The Cooper School has a culture of high standards that is supported by the University of Pittsburgh. The principles of learning: Clear Expectations, Organization for Effort, Academic Rigor, Accountable Talk, and Socializing for Intelligence, which supports our daily instructional programs (Resnick & Fink, 2001). We also incorporated Brian Cambourne's "Conditions for Learning" to encourage high expectations for student work and differentiated instruction (Cambourne, 2002). In addition, a schoolwide philosophy and instructional practice through Keene's (2006) ideas on thinking strategies were consistently and rigorously implemented.

Parents and students highly valued the school and showed a great deal of respect for everyone. Teachers worked closely and productively together with students and families to develop instruction and interventions that supported the whole child. The Cooper School strived to maximize each individual student's opportunity to do well.

This chapter analyzes the mentoring process as it was used at Cooper Elementary School. Through mentoring, commitment, acceptance, communication, and inspiration, the school was guided into becoming a high-performing organization. Leaders and coaches provided mentoring and coaching to the staff. Planning and collaborative time to mentor and coach individual teachers was established. Assessments of student performance to improve classroom instruction and student outcomes were included as part of the process. Classes were rescheduled so that students received reading and math instruction earlier in the school day. Mentors created and expanded learning communities in the school to raise expectations for students' success and to create a resourceful atmosphere of support.

CREATING A POSITIVE LEARNING CULTURE

Before the school received the National Blue Ribbon award, the guidance counselor wanted to create a positive environment for special needs children who were having emotional challenges in the school. She assembled a group of thirty school personnel members—who included teachers, secretaries, paraprofessionals, kitchen staff, school safety officers, and the custodial staff—to work together to act as mentors for these highly selective students. The counselor gave each mentor one student with a list of positive activities for developing mentor-mentee relationships.

The program realized a noticeable difference in the children who participated. Also, a mutual respect and strong home-school connection developed as a result of this mentoring program. The school's personnel became a strong support mechanism for these troubled students by involving them in extracurricular activities during the weekend, taking them to museums, parks, and the movies, as well as helping them after school with additional academic support. Hence, the mentorship program changed the school's environment by fostering these meaningful relationships between students and adults.

When developing relationships and culture, it was very important to create a warm and caring environment built on trust and engaging conversations, where everyone played the role of a major contributor. Students, parents, administrators, teachers, paraprofessionals, guidance counselors, coaches, psychologists, social workers, and support staff were all major decision makers in the organization. Also, community members were a part of the collaborative practices that changed the trajectory of the school.

Rutherford (2005) stated,

> In such a school there would be clearly articulated, commonly held and acted upon beliefs. Those beliefs would value student learning and professional growth of staff in the interest of student learning. Acting on those beliefs means that in such a school, teachers seek to be mentors and actively pursue the learning of knowledge and the acquisition of skills identified critical for successful mentors. They are analytical and reflective about the impact of their actions on the professional growth of the teachers with whom they are working and use that analysis in reflection to make adjustments to their mentoring practice. (p. 4)

A climate of intellectual development evolved as the principal gave very close attention to the nature and quality of interactions between administrators, coaches, teachers, parents, and students. All stakeholders, in time, exhibited a high level of respect for students, parents, colleagues, and themselves. When people knew that they were valued, respected, and appreciated, they rose to the occasion to do well. It was prophesized by the principal that students, parents, and teachers were the best and brightest people in the world—and they lived up to that mantra.

Mentoring principals, Salazar (2008)

> built a culture of commitment, collegiality, mutual respect and stability. There is a belief system that supports peer coaching, collaboration, trust, shared

responsibility, and continuous learning by the adults in the school. This requires on-going development of people skills in making fact based decisions, working with diverse groups, resolving conflicts and using effective strategies to build consensus. (p. 49)

Rutherford (2005) expressed concepts of strong mentorship practices needed in school improvement, as illustrated by the following attributes:

1. Teachers were well versed in pedagogy and content knowledge and were able to gather student work that demonstrated standard-level mastery.
2. During team meetings, members were positive contributors and understood their interdependent role in working together to achieve the common good for all children.
3. Administrators, coaches, and teachers communicated timely and effective information to students, parents, and appropriate staff concerning students' performance and progress.
4. Team members persistently explored ways to support all colleagues to help students accomplish academic success.

These communications and structures were put into place to motivate and inspire the school community. Engaging conversations with all constituents—through monthly schoolwide learning walks, weekly grade meetings, and daily common grade-level preparation periods, daily inspirational message boards, weekly newsletters, monthly assembly programs, and weekly parent workshops—created shared responsibility, meaningful relationships, and a dynamic learning environment for all. These experiences, as mentioned above, permeated throughout the school to transform all participants and create a spirit of intellectual excellence.

RAISING HIGH EXPECTATIONS

The structure of leadership and the roles of the principal have been significant in changing the expectations that teachers have for students. Using a collaborative team-based approach that consisted of the principal's cabinet, grade-level learning communities, the school leadership team, and curriculum and professional development teams created a collegial and nurturing learning environment. These key groups consisted of a facilitator and six to nine members who get together regularly.

The overarching cluster was the principal's cabinet. All teams nurtured the leadership group. It was led by the school principal and was comprised of the assistant principal, union representative, teacher center specialist, intervention coordinator, and the literacy, math, and early childhood coaches. Their primary focus established policies and programs, formulated community-based relationships, and selected targeted resources to improve student achievement.

The grade-level teams were guided by coaches who gathered weekly to discuss data and instructional strategies, plan and revise units of study, create curriculum maps, develop lab sites for each grade, share best practices, use a wide range of data to support student learners, and set measurable long-term and interim goals.

The school leadership team consisted of half parents and half staff, who met monthly to discuss school activities, assess progress, develop initiatives, and review and analyze the comprehensive education plan. The curriculum and professional development team consisted of all coaches, administration, and a representative from each learning community. Their main goals were to design strategically targeted curriculum and professional development that met the needs of both teachers and students.

The role of the principal was to serve as a transformative, inspirational, instructional, and collegial leader—mentor—who collaborated with teams of teachers and staff to implement effective instructional programs and practices that best served the learning community. As one student said, "Our principal believes we can do anything so we work and study hard to achieve."

The mission of the school provided maximum opportunities for all children to become capable and concerned citizens of the world. We created an environment of high expectations and standards that challenged our students to reach their maximum level of performance in all academic areas. Thus, the instructional program supported multiple intelligences and different learning styles and helped foster opportunities to create a nurturing, supportive learning environment that promoted excellence as well as a love of learning.

Our belief in Brian Cambourne's Conditions of Learning and Lauren Resnick's Principles of Learning supported our mission and vision for teaching and learning. We also believed that to educate children, we must address the academic, social, emotional, and psychological needs of the child. Children learn best when they are engaged in meaningful real-world, collaborative experiences that are challenging, rigorous, and creative; children learn best in a caring community where they feel safe to take risks and to reflect on and to participate in their learning. Thus, given the right support and sufficient time, every child can learn, and learning occurs best when every person who touches the life of a child works as partners in the education of the child (Cambourne, 2002).

The school developed learning walks around Cambourne's Conditions of Learning and Resnick's Principles of Learning. On a monthly basis, one teacher from each grade was selected to participate on a walk-through to view best practices on a specific instructional practice and topic. During the learning walk, each grade modeled the same teaching practice and topic for participants to view. Approximately six classes were visited for about four to eight minutes. After viewing a modeled lesson, the teachers gathered outside for a brief discussion using a protocol that allowed the teacher to give warm and cool feedback. Warm feedback included compliments that the teacher shared based on the observation, and cool feedback was given with questions that the teacher had in regard to the observation.

At the end of the walk-through, teachers met in the teacher center to synthesize the experience by sharing their thoughts on the learning walk experience. The model teachers were then asked to join the learning walk participants so that they could share their warm and cool feedback and engage in meaningful conversations about best instructional practices.

The learning walks were a major factor in the school's improvement. These activities put everyone on the "same page" about instruction and student achievement. With this kind of practice, the school virtually eliminated the achievement gap with a student population that included immigrants from the Caribbean with limited English proficiency (LEP) and low-income children of color living in impoverished conditions.

On the 2005 to 2006 state exams, 53 percent of the students in grades three, four, and five attained levels 3 and 4 in mathematics and 37 percent attained levels 3 and 4 in English Language Arts (ELA). Those scores increased in 2008–2009 to 97 percent of students scoring at or above level in math and 87 percent scoring at or above level in ELA. In addition, a major milestone occurred in 2009 when the fourth-grade students made the most gains of any other fourth grade in the state of New York in both ELA and mathematics statewide exams!

What makes the school unique is its collegial teaching and learning environment, the extensive use of data-driven instruction, the cohesive learning atmosphere, the strategically targeted professional development, and a reflective instructional community that embraces all constituents. In addition, what set this school apart from the others was its academically rigorous schedule and program design, which gave teachers and students three to four hours of uninterrupted instructional time and daily common preparation periods in which teachers were able to hold grade-level meetings to discuss student data, instructional strategies, and curriculum. This kind of work has become a tradition in the school and has greatly contributed to the high student achievement.

IMPROVING INSTRUCTION

Beginning 2004–2005, the school formed learning communities that included coaches, grade-level leaders, and teachers from each grade level. Through these learning communities, the school continued to foster a tradition of data-driven decision making. This changed how teachers viewed students' needs and how they delivered instruction. Academic goals were set for all students based on data beginning in prekindergarten. The strengths and weaknesses were made transparent to students and parents, leading to increased student engagement and success.

This kind of focused instruction, professional development, and constant review of data were the driving factors that led the school to success and made it worthy of becoming a Blue Ribbon School of Excellence. The administrators, coaches, teachers, paraprofessionals, parents, and students were excited about the teaching and learning that emerged in the classroom environment.

Each student has his or her own learning style. While some students learn by seeing, others learn by hearing and others learn by doing. To create an effective learning environment that meets all of these different needs, our teachers used a variety of instructional methods firmly grounded in coaching and mentoring. These methods engaged students, helping them to truly become learners. Teachers were also encouraged to become learners through rich professional development opportunities in and outside of school. There were three full-time coaches available to mentor teachers and model instruction. They worked exclusively with teachers to improve practice for greater student achievement. This is one reason why the school retained its teachers and has a very low teacher turnaround. The average teacher had fifteen years of experience.

INSTRUCTIONAL MODEL

Instruction was developed through the workshop model. The workshop model consisted of whole-class instruction, small-group instruction, individualized instruction, and lesson summary through whole-class participation. The workshop model provided explicit instruction, demonstration via the mini lesson, independent practice that allows students to practice the strategy taught, and partnership work. During differentiated instruction the teacher observes, teaches, and assesses student learning through individualized work, small-group work, and one-on-one conferences. The teacher during this stage is afforded the opportunity to differentiate instruction through conferences with students independently, or by doing guided and/or strategy group instruction.

Within our instruction, students' learning styles and multiple intelligences are addressed using drama, role-playing, music, and art. One of our targeted subgroups met weekly as the Boys Writing Club with a published author to enhance their writing and social skills. Technology, Title I reading, and math were also used to supplement instruction to targeted students.

The curriculum was enhanced by a wide range of creative and cultural activities as well as frequent visits to places of interest. The school performed *The Jungle Book* on Broadway at the Victory Theater with the support of a grant from the Disney Corporation. In addition to this program, the school implemented on-site visits from theater and dance groups to continue to enhance our students' learning experiences.

Assembly programs were implemented in which students were awarded for perfect attendance, student of the month, most improved, and work well done. A student council was formed as a vehicle for students to mentor and encourage each other to strive toward high achievement. The school's Saturday Academy provided academic support for students and was a valuable resource in differentiating instruction and providing needed support for struggling students. The instructional methods that we adopted through coaching and mentoring contributed to higher performance academically for all students.

RAISING ACHIEVEMENT

The Cooper School participates in the state assessment system with performance levels ranging from 1 through 4 for both ELA and mathematics. Level 1 means students are functioning far below the assessed state standard grade-level expectations, level 2 means students are partially meeting state standards, level 3 means students are meeting grade-level standards expectations, and level 4 means students are exceeding grade-level standards expectations. Students' skills are assessed through students answering multiple choice and extended response ELA and math items.

The school made significant gains in ELA and mathematics in grades three through five over a five-year period. The assessment results were used to set measurable interim and long-term school goals, class goals, and individual student goals. The administration, coaches, and teachers work collaboratively to analyze data to understand clearly what each student knows, which enables us to monitor student progress. Analysis of data also revealed support needed for our subgroups (ELL and special education population) to help them achieve academic success.

Every classroom teacher had a data binder that held individual students' assessment results as well as whole-class information. Analysis of reports from binders showed students' strengths and weaknesses, guided teachers' decisions on instruction, and supported the formulation of small groups and one-on-one conferencing. In-depth analysis of student data afforded all of the students opportunities to be provided differentiated instruction.

Decisions were also made to target students for additional support through intervention sessions, extended day, after school, Saturday, and vacation programs and lunchtime work sessions. Accurate records were kept of student progress for each service provided. Upon reviewing students' progress, teachers came together to evaluate the effectiveness of each program and to plan for future teaching and learning.

In addition, instructional coaches facilitated teachers' development of curriculum maps based on state standards, practice tests, and conferring notes. These maps were used as guides to differentiate instruction across all subject areas.

Charts and graphs of goals and progress toward our target were displayed in classrooms and corridors to make goals transparent to all of the school community. Students, teachers, and parents had formal and informal discussions about the data and the support needed to achieve goals. Through conferring and consistent feedback from teachers, students were actively involved in setting personal goals and knowing their responsibilities toward achieving them. At grade-level meetings, teachers reflected on student and schoolwide targets.

COMMUNICATING ASSESSMENT RESULTS

Everyone in the school community had high expectations for student performance and a responsibility to help students achieve high standards. The Cooper School developed a comprehensive strategy for communicating student performance and standardized test scores to everyone in the learning community.

The principal collaborated weekly with the cabinet, which included the assistant principal, math coach, literacy coach, teacher center specialist, early childhood literacy coach, union representative, and the intervention coordinator. The school leadership team that was comprised of 50 percent parents and 50 percent staff assembled monthly and worked collaboratively with the principal, focusing on the implementation of the development of the Comprehensive Education Plan (CEP). The administration attended monthly parent association meetings to report on student performance and school goals outlined in the CEP.

The administrators, teachers, and support staff were committed to communicating student achievement to parents and community support organizations on a regular basis. The principal corresponds through a monthly grade-level newsletter, parent calendar, daily announcements via school messenger telephone communications, and letters keeping parents apprised of the school's activities and information. Bimonthly progress letters were sent to parents informing them of the current level of performance of their child and specific activities on how to support them at home.

The school also articulated to the entire community a greater understanding of what was expected of students, parents, teachers, administrators, and staff. In addition, teacher and parent surveys were given three times a year to assess progress and identify questions or concerns teachers and parents may have had in reference to school activities, curriculum, homework, school environment, safety, and more. This information had consistently proven to be very valuable in our overall school academic/curriculum development, workshop planning, and general school communications as well as parent, teacher, and student engagement.

CONCLUSION

In any school organization, instruction is the key to success and high student achievement. Cheliotes and Reilly's (2010) concepts of *mentor-leaders and coachlike leaders* give educators like the teachers in the Cooper School the support needed to excel. The school leader took on a "mentor-leader" style in relationships with the staff. The principal was a partner and collaborator with all staff members. She understood the new leadership role that demonstrated transparency, openness, passion, respect of ideas and opinions, collaboration, and "coachlike leaders" to imagine teachers' abilities to strengthen and exceed. They saw themselves as partners and grew through coaching conversations. The principal was perceived as a partner and not a supervisor. It was "coachlike leader" relationships that helped all school personnel at the Cooper School to excel and succeed.

In an effort to build a strong community, all adults in the school were responsible for providing support to all teachers and support staff. That support addressed the four crucial areas of departments in terms of personal, professional, logistical, and instructional support. The principal and coaches supported basic systems to create a positive, supportive, and meaningful environment that fostered collaboration and cooperation.

The significance of growth and progress in the organization came to light by the creation of a culture in which all educators understood the value and importance of mentoring as a natural component of the school. A positive demonstration of this collaboration was the back-to-school parent-teacher conferences at which everyone was apprised of the steadfast belief of how children learn, the overall history of the school, and how each member plays a role in the implementation of school improvement and exemplary academic excellence.

The staff was given clear directives in regard to conducting lab site visits, learning walks, and grade meetings. The school environment was organized to build strong collaboration and planning sessions. Meetings were purpose-fully focused on content, and shared leadership was an integral part of the process. Mentoring was a part of the school improvement plan, with indica-tors and benchmarks for student achievement; teachers, lead teachers, and coaches' success; parent involvement; curriculum and instruction; scheduling and programming; and data assessment.

Daily provisions were made through scheduling and programing to accommodate and facilitate coaching to facilitate teams and to plan, prepare, observe, and reflect upon instructional practices. Responsibilities of teachers and coaches were reduced to maximize their time together. Frequent moni-toring enabled key staff to discuss progress and offer any necessary support.

Best practices of teaching and learning were aligned for optimum student success. Coaches led grade meetings, supporting staff in sharing units of study, lesson plans, and learning standards and individualized student assess-ment practices. Coaches served on the cabinet for building-level support and for instructional, curriculum, and assessment planning.

In conclusion, Rutherford (2005) states it best:

> The focus of mentor practice for our school was to lead teachers to engage in their professional practice with the following perspectives in mind: a sense of self efficacy; a focus on clearly articulated standards of learning; an ever grow-ing repertoire of skills for teaching and assessing diverse learners; a passion for engaging all students in the learning process; the use of data to make and assess instructional decisions; a mission to promote high standards and expectations for students and educators; and a commitment to collaborate with colleagues and parents. (p. 22)

The school thus worked in accordance with the African proverb, "It takes a village to raise a child," and to improve a school to achieve maximum excellence.

REFERENCES

Cambourne, B. (2002). The conditions of learning: Is learning natural? *Reading Teacher 55* (8), 758–62.

Cheliotes, L., & Reilly, M. (2010). *Coaching conversations*. Thousand Oaks, CA: Corwin Press.

Keene, E. (2006). *Assessing comprehension thinking strategies*. Huntington Beach, CA: Shell Education.

Keene, E. O., & Zimmerman, S. (2007). *Mosaic of thought: Teaching comprehension in a reader's workshop*. Portsmouth, NH: Heinemann Educational Books.

Resnick, L. B., & Fink, E. (2001). Developing principals as instructional leaders. *Phi Delta Kappan 8*, 598–610.

Rowley, J. (2006). *Becoming a high-performance mentor: A guide to reflection and action.* Thousand Oaks, CA: Corwin Press.

Rutherford, P. (2005). *The 21st century mentor's handbook: Creating a culture for learning.* Alexandria, VA: Just Ask Publication.

Salazar, P. (2008). *High-impact leadership for high-impact schools: The actions that matter most.* New York: Eye on Education.

Smylie, M. (2010). *Continuous school improvement.* Thousand Oaks, CA: Corwin Press.

Weingartner, C. (2009). *Principal mentoring.* Thousand Oaks, CA: Corwin Press.

Chapter 3

Climate Controller

Principals Creating Optimal Environments for Teacher Development

Dagoberto Artiles

School climate starts with the human and material composition of the school. The interactions between and including the human and material entities determine the quality of the school climate, learning, and life. Tableman (2004) stated that school climate was "the physical and psychological aspects of the school that provide the preconditions necessary for teaching and learning to take place" (p. 2). In other words, school climate refers to the quality and character of interactions among the people in a school building. The role of the school principal can be viewed in two perspectives: as *managerial* or *instructional* in the way they consider school climate. From the managerial point of view, the principal manages in an environment of control, distrust, and fear of challenges. And from the instructional point of view, the principal leads in a climate that promotes collaboration and growth.

This chapter analyzes the relationship between school climate and effectiveness of teacher mentoring programs with the principal acting as climate controller. The research on school climate is limited as virtually no information exists on the idea of referring to the school principal as a climate controller. The reference made to *school climate* in this chapter does not deal with school environments related to health issues, such as the physical environment and air quality of the school building that can have a negative impact on everyone's health and on the learning process.

Instead, this chapter looks at the school climate as the quality of the interrelations that takes place among academic standards, expectations, and support affecting the groups of people who work in the school building. Zullig, Koopman, Patton, and Ubbes (2010) indicated that although the construct of school climate can be traced back over a one hundred years (Perry, 1908), "the scientific study of school climate was not undertaken until the 1950s with the birth of organizational climate research" (p. 140). Cohen, McCabe,

Michelli, and Pickeral (2009) proposed that school climate "refers to the quality and character of school life, based on patterns of people's experiences of school life and reflects norms, goals, values, interpersonal relationships, teaching and learning practices, and organizational structures" (p. 10).

Furthermore, Zullig et al. (2010) talked about March and Simon (1958) and Argyris (1958) as the creators of "organization climate" when they began to analyze businesses and other organizations in an attempt to correlate the influences of an organizational environment on such outcomes as morale, productivity, profitability, and turnover (p. 140). As Zullig et al. (2010) stated, March and Simon (1958) and Argyris (1958) "attempted to correlate the influences of an organizational environment to such outcomes as morale, productivity, and turnover" (p. 140).

Research about the influence of an organizational environment over its members continued through the 1960s and 1970s, leading to the association of the organizational environment to school climate and the climate's effects on student outcomes in schools (effectiveness). Brookover, Schweitzer, Schneider, Beady, Flood, and Wisenbaker (1978) indicated that the concept of "school climate" has been used in many different ways (p. 302).

Brookover et al. (1978) continued by stating that the composition of the student body—as measured by socioeconomic status, race, or other composition variables—has been frequently used as a measure for school climate. Others have used indictors of student personality or characteristics of school organization as proxies for school climate (Anderson, 1970; Oreilly, 1975). Brookover et al. (1978) conceived of school academic climate as follows:

> The school social climate encompasses a composite of variables as defined and perceived by the members of this group. These factors may be broadly conceived as the norms of the social system and expectations held for various members as perceived by the members of the group and communicated to members of the group. These two general dimensions—norms and expectations—are theoretically highly related. Norms tend to be expressed in the common beliefs concerning the appropriate forms of behaviors for members of the social system. Norms and expectations involve both the definitions of appropriate behavior expressed by others in the system, and the perceptions of these expectations as understood by members of the group. (p. 303)

This definition clearly establishes that school climate can be defined as the quality of the interactions that takes place between: (1) academic standards, (2) expectation, and (3) mutual support. As a result, a climate controller can be defined as leader who is able to establish high expectations along with matching support to create an environment of high academic achievement. The hard part about being a climate controller is maintaining these three areas—working at full capacity consistently. Furthermore, the quality of these interactions is not determined by the makeup of the student body. Brookover et al. (1978) stated that "school climate is not synonymous with the social composition of its student body; and therefore, climate is not adequately measured by composition variables" (p. 303).

Notably, Cohen et al. (2009) implied that school climate is "the quality and character of school life that are . . . based on patterns of people's experience of school life and reflects norms, goals, values, interpersonal relationships, teaching and learning practices, and organizational structures" (p. 182). These interactions will be such that strangers who walk into the school building will instantly sense a feeling about the school, which could be called "climate." As we currently know, principals have a direct influence on two functions of the school, as evaluators and coach/mentors. Kelley (1981) indicated that "a common assumption has been that school administrators should focus their efforts to improve climate on improving staff morale. While this assumed relationships between satisfaction (morale) and productivity (achievement) are seductive, research has consistently shown that it is neither predictive nor causal" (p. 180).

EVOLUTION FROM INSTRUCTIONAL LEADER TO CLIMATE CONTROLLER

Every school has a climate that sets it apart from other schools and affects behavior and feelings of teachers and students toward the school. The principal, as the leader responsible for maintaining the school climate at the optimal performance level, is directly involved in making his/her school operate apart from others. As the requirements and benchmarks of our public education system have become better defined and more specific, the need for the innovation of current practice is nonnegotiable. A generation of research has provided evidence demonstrating that effective school leaders attending to the needs of the school organizations improve academic achievement goals (Black, 2010, p. 437).

Schools are social organizations, and Gunbayi (2007) stated that "within school organizations there are students, teachers, administrators, and many kinds of service personnel. Members of each of these groups occupy distinctive positions and are expected to behave in certain ways" (p. 70). Clearly, the relationships among many kinds of people in schools are varied and complex. Only if those relationships are understood and generally accepted by others can the school organization function effectively.

Creating an environment that provides adequate support to teachers requires a leader with the ability to change the attitudes and behaviors of the members who function within the school environment. Moos (1979) concluded that "educational settings can and do make a difference in students' lives" (p. 43). This difference can be for better of for worse. Students, teachers, parents, and principals are correct in assuming that their choices and policies matter—and that the educational settings they select and create have varied impacts. It is clear that school climate does make a difference in what happens to the people who lead, teach, and learn in a particular school environment.

The idea behind becoming a climate controller is not to adapt the attitude of leadership, but to focus on how to allow the people in the school environment to grow as staff by demonstrating freedom of creativity and innovation. The attribute to "serve others" is not simply serving in the sense of *doing things for others*. The leaders' focus is to make the persons served more competent to meet their own needs and to be better equipped to serve the organization and society in general (Black, 2010, p. 440). The main goal of the climate controller is to allow the people in the organization to become more *independent*—and not more dependent on the leader.

Visionary, creative, knowledgeable, principled, and inspiring educational leaders are vital to creating and fostering a positive school environment to help meet public education goals in the twenty-first century (Black, 2010, p. 337). Climate controllers value less defensive strategies and are more participatory in the quest to create a stimulating environment. As twenty-first-century leaders, the climate controller is expected to "become both more and less," as explained below:

(1) Become less a controller and disciplinarian and more a team builder and cooperative problem solver, (2) become less a motivator and persuader and more a climate builder, (3) becoming less a firefighter and more a planner, (4) become less a conservator, resister, and preserver of the culture and more an innovator, a creator, and a quiet revolutionary, and (5) become less of a role and more a person.

The school climate is not a permanent condition; instead, it is fluid and ever changing. As a climate controller, the school principal is responsible for providing maintenance to the factors that influence the school climate.

SCHOOL CLIMATE THAT LEADS TO EFFECTIVE TEACHER'S MENTORING

Development of a comprehensive system of teacher mentoring enhances a school's ability to promote academic success and professional maturity. Mentoring is a supportive, personalized, long-term relationship between an experienced mentor and their less experienced mentee. According to Newton

(1987, p. 28), seven variables are essential for the development of an effective teacher mentoring program at the school level, including:

1. adequate timelines: for developing and implementing plans;
2. participation of teachers, administrators, educational organizations, and community members in planning and implementing programs;
3. development of a fair, and perceived as fair, selection process with systematic procedures that are clearly articulated and adhered to in practice;
4. provision of training for mentor teachers to enable them to effectively carry out their new role (e.g., knowledge of adult learning theory, team building, and the role of a change agent; skills in group leadership and facilitation, group problem solving, observation and conferencing, role modeling and demonstration, networking and collaboration, coaching, and counseling);
5. provision of ongoing administrative support;
6. availability of sufficient funding to cover the costs inherent in the program as well as to study its effectiveness;
7. provision of time, as built into the schedules of teachers and mentors, that allows each to observe the other teaching and to confer with one another after observations; and assignment of teacher to a mentor located in the same building and, if possible, teaching the same subject/grade.

Thus, an essential component of an effective mentoring program is the well-planned selection process of mentors. Mentors should not be selected through a process of assignment or seniority; instead, we should create the environment where qualified mentor candidates will come forward and volunteer for the assignment.

Ganser (2002) stated the following:

All members of the school community should understand how a new teacher mentoring program operates, especially non-mentoring veteran teachers and teachers serving in leadership positions (e.g., grade level leaders and department chairpersons). Within the school, the professional staff (e.g., guidance counselor and school social worker), clerical staff, and maintenance staff should also understand how the mentor program works. (p. 6)

Other stakeholders who should also understand how the mentoring program works are students, parents, board education members, and community organizations. Garsen (2002, p. 6) indicated that principals should know the answers to many questions about the mentoring program in their schools, including the answer to these six queries:

- Does the program serve only beginning teachers at the very start of their career, or does it also serve experienced teachers who are new to the school or grade level?
- What are the criteria and processes used to select veteran teachers to serve as mentors?
- How are mentors assigned to new teachers?
- Are mentors provided with released time with their mentees or to observe them teaching?
- If so, what are the arrangements to make this happen?
- How are conflicts between a mentor and mentee handled?

The inner workings of a mentor program should not only be common knowledge but also not be limited to the mentor and the mentee. The principal as the climate controller is responsible for sharing valuable information about the program as often as possible, allowing the principal to show support for the program and staff and how they adjust to the changing school climate.

Schools have the ability to create and model mentoring programs according to the strengths of the school climate. People in education tend to believe that mentoring is the spontaneous interaction among the members of the school. However, Daloz (1999) indicated that what makes the difference is the mentor's willingness to care (p. 20). Daloz's position gives emphasis to the *value-added functions* of the mentor and the role that the mentor plays in the process of the mentorship and the mentoring program.

Zellers, Howard, and Barcic (2008) indicated that mentoring programs call for a process of "cultural synergism" in which the setting is transformed to embrace the strengths of collective values and interactions (e.g., male-female, minority-majority), and thus mentoring is reenvisioned beyond "the white male club" (p. 562). As the process of the mentoring program is developed, the principal must also consider the challenges of recommendations and remediation systems within the program.

The new realities of our fast-moving and technologically influenced educational system may often require individuals to seek guidance. Zellers et al. (2008) stated:

> One mentor is no longer adequate to meet the full complement of another's technical and personal needs in the context of modern society. Dynamic organizational change, increased specialization and innovation, and the acceleration of technological advances prescribe a new mentoring paradigm in which mentoring relationships are pluralistic and reciprocal. (p. 563)

This new paradigm can only be made possible in a school climate in which mentoring relationships work in harmony and are synchronized to maximize time and effort. School climate—that is constantly monitored and adjusted to allow for the highest levels of interaction among mentors and mentees—can often lead to the availability of a series of mentors instead of just one.

The context of the school and its culture that are developed and nurtured becomes the difference maker in how successful is the mentoring program. Teachers, who were there with low morale, negative attitudes, and poor over-all environment, may often not get the opportunity to reflect and understand the unique challenges of effective teaching. As Tillman (2005) stated, it is important that principals (1) serve as developers and nurturers, (2) help new teachers understand the school culture, and (3) encourage them to transfer and adjust what they have learned in their teacher education programs and previous jobs to the current school context (p. 613).

Principals need to understand that not all teachers' personal experiences and education background are sufficient enough to overcome the challenges of the school setting. Tillman (2005) indicated that mentoring can be used to help first-year teachers acquire the skills to think critically about their experiences as well as their professional and personal competence in the school community (p. 613).

Mentoring programs are a means to provide teachers the assistance they need as they develop their skills set. Ganser (2002) stated that at the "heart of every successful new teacher mentor program is the relationship between mentors and their mentees" (p. 8). Principals can support this relationship in two important ways. As Ganser (2002) indicated:

> The first is to act on the recognition that effective mentoring is time-intensive by freeing mentors from other professional responsibilities whenever possible. A second absolutely essential way for principals to support the mentoring rela-tionship is by respecting the trust and confidentiality between the teacher and mentor. (p. 8)

While mentors are a great source of information, principals must respect confidentiality and refrain from overly inquiring information about the process.

IMPACTS OF SCHOOL CLIMATE ON MENTORS AND MENTEES

Principals as "climate controllers" are responsible for assessing the support mechanisms that are already in place at the building level for new teachers. Ganser (2002) stated that to avoid a wasteful duplication of services or the unintended "drifting" or preexisting responsibilities for the well-being of new teachers to the mentor program (and, more specifically, to the mentor), principals can facilitate a new teacher support audit at their school (p. 9). The principal must first collaborate with experienced teachers and district-level colleagues regarding any support services that already are available to teachers within the school and at the district level. Ganser (2002) talked about three major steps in identifying the support services and resources available at the school and district level in order to minimize waste and duplication (p. 10).

The first step is to brainstorm *with* veteran teachers, relatively new teachers, and central office personnel (e.g., staff development, human resources, curriculum, and instruction) about sources of assistance for new teachers that already exist within the school and the school district, excluding a formal mentoring program. The second step is to determine the sources of assistance that already exist outside of the school and school district (e.g., teachers' professional associations, and local or state chapters of professional organizations). The third step is to consider how a formal mentor program can be designed so as to complement these preexisting sources of assistance (Ganser, 2002, p. 10).

The first week of September is very exciting for new teachers as they start a new career or simply move to another district or school. Everything is in place, and we find ourselves surrounded by returning teachers, greeting each other and recalling their summer vacations. For new teachers, however, this is a nerve-racking time since they are not yet aware of the new school or program difficulties and the challenges that they will encounter as they undertake a new career.

Lataille (2005) stated that "after a quick explanation of local procedures, new teachers are frequently left very much on their own" (p. 60). Experienced teachers who are usually better suited to mentor less experienced teachers become preoccupied with their own responsibilities, often forgetting that they were in a possible position to be helpful, as the new teachers next door may be new in their careers and or locations. Teaching is an incredibly isolated career, in which professional and personal interactions are minimal.

Principals should realize that teachers—even with some experience who change school, grade levels, or subjects within the same school—often encounter the same challenges as new teachers. With this in mind, good principals acting as climate controllers often manage to create a school environment with the flexibility to assist all teachers in need. Lataille (2005) indicated that the mentoring process needs to be separated from the evaluation process (p. 61). This detachment allows teachers to be more candid and open with their mentors and freer to discuss those pedagogical areas where they sense they are weak or deficient. It also encourages self-improvement without any fear of experiencing negative consequences affecting employment

(Lataille, 2005, p. 61). This approach should not be limited to new teachers. In fact, experienced teachers must be reassured that the mentoring process will be conducted with fidelity and objectivity.

The educational process of children involves multiple elements; however, the main elements are the interactions between the teachers and the students. Teachers construct specific learning environments and requirements for their students, introduce learning requirements, and evaluate the outcome of this process when grading their pupils. Cummings (2011) indicated that to establish a cohesive work environment, professional development programs for teachers should reflect this paradigm.

Teachers, however, are neither children nor adolescents. They are adult learners, and thus professional development programs for teachers should address the characteristics of adult learning (p. 19). Teachers' abilities to conduct self-evaluations that affect their own level of efficacy are central to understanding the complexities of adult learning. Cummings (2011, p. 19) further indicated that one characteristic of adult learning is self-directed learning. And from early perspectives on self-directed learning, proposed in 1975, Malcolm Knowles characterized adult learners doing for themselves what they do for their students—that is, "climate setting, engaging in learning activities, and evaluating learning outcomes" (pp. 34–37).

SCHOOL CLIMATE FOR ADULT LEARNERS

Teachers must also look at themselves as adult learners for the mentoring program to be successful. The principal, as the "lead climate controller," is charged with the role of creating an environment in which teachers feel comfortable becoming adult learners and take on self-directed learning activities as a result of their interactions with their mentors. Knowles (1975, pp. 37–38) listed three aspects concerning self-directed learning; these are:

- that adult students in regular self-directed learning programs would be concerned that they get the required content to pass their exams, get certified, obtain licenses, get accepted into other institutions, or get jobs
- that self-directed learners may be concerned with the grades they will receive or the status of their promotions upon completion of their self-directed learning projects
- that self-directed learning is a process structure, whereas they (the students) have been used to a content structure. Knowles (1975) insisted on the necessity of a *facilitator* to guide the process of self-directed learners through this foreign-to-them process structure. Therefore, facilitators should be in charge of the self-directed learning process.

The mentor or the facilitator is thus charged with guiding the process of the mentorship and providing specifics to support to the mentee. Mentors have to be able to create and design opportunities for the mentees during the process. These opportunities should be influenced by the learning expectations that have been established by the school environment.

Walking into an auditorium full of people smiling and hugging each other after a well-deserved summer vacation is comforting and motivating. Looking around at the clean floors, neatly arranged classrooms, and new textbooks may give new teachers a false sense of security. Thus, Schwille (2008) and Feiman-Nemser (1998, 2001) coined the term *educative mentoring* to distinguish this kind of mentoring of novices and new teachers from the more conventional supervisory approach. The concept of educative mentoring is based on learning theories that depict the learner as an active participant in the learning process (p. 140). In this climate, mentoring will be based on the premise that the mentee will interact with his/her environment (and mentor) in the manner that is a suitable path to produce growth.

Mentoring programs in school climate that lead to growth will be targeted and precise in nature. The process of mentoring will, thus, be grounded in the mission of creating opportunities for learning and a better grasp of the art and science of teaching, and of teaching and learning to teach. Mentoring in highly effective school climates goes beyond the emotional and psychological platforms of teaching; instead, mentoring takes on a role of support and resource allocation to create the highest form of learning opportunities for the mentees. Schwille (2008, p. 141) mentioned that learning to teach requires more than just hand holding; it demands involvement in, and an understanding of, the intellectual nature and process of teaching and learning to teach. Learning to teach can only be accomplished by engaging the mentee in the authentic tasks of teaching.

Mentoring structures that are designed to engage the mentee in authentic teaching experiences—processes by which they learn to make effective decisions about curriculum, assessment validity, and instructional practice—are fundamental. Green (2006) indicated that mentor teachers are commonly charged with providing beginning teachers with structured means of examining their decisions that affect classroom practices. Through a structured system of support, beginning teachers have opportunities to reflect on their lesson planning, delivery of instruction, and use of various instructional strategies (p. 8). Parker, Ndoy, and Imig (2009) explained that while it is vital to offer mentoring to novice teachers, it is equally as important to seek ways to improve the *quality* of these experiences to help new educators become more effective and to reduce beginning teachers' attrition (p. 330). Mentoring is fundamental to the beliefs of lifelong learning.

Participation in the mentoring program alone does not guarantee success and growth on the part of the mentee. As indicated by Ganser (2002), success as a teacher can be attributed to three factors:

> The first factor includes the knowledge, skills, and dispositions that new teachers bring to their work—what they already know about good teaching as they walk through the school house door and what they are able to do to put that knowledge to use. The second factor includes workplace conditions, such as the numbers and abilities of children in classes, classroom resources, and curricular and instructional support. The third factor reflects all elements of induction support for new teachers, including mentoring, but everything else as well, such as staff orientation meetings, special meetings and services for new teachers, and the all-important culture of the school as related to the transition of a new teacher from "outsider" to "insider." (p. 10)

Acknowledging these conditions with new teachers or new hires, principals as climate controllers should work to create a common interpretation regarding what is realistic and what is not realistic to expect about new staff members of the school community. For example, if a newly hired teacher is weak in some essential skills, it is probably unreasonable and unfair to expect the mentoring program and the mentor to eliminate the deficiency. Therefore, it is unwise to hire a teacher who otherwise would not be employed just because a new mentor program exists (Ganser, 2002, p. 10).

LESSONS LEARNED

Mentoring programs for new and existing teachers are basic components of professional development strategies across the educational field. Formally organized programs, linking new teachers with experienced veteran teachers serving as their mentors, emerged in the 1970s (Ganser, 2002, p. 3). The commonality and appreciation for mentoring programs today can be credited in part to the shortage of teachers that the school system is and was experiencing. However, mentoring programs are only one way to address quality teachers' support services and resources alignment.

Smith and Ingersoll (2004) indicated that the teaching occupation has not had the kind of structured induction and initiation processes common to many white-collar occupations and characteristic of many traditional professions such as for lawyers and doctors (p. 681). Ironically, the interactions that teachers are more exposed to—which is with their students—are often conducted in day-to-day isolation from their adult fellow colleagues.

The notion of "school" in this chapter is not really a building, but rather a setting or environment of education that contains a group of people who go there every day and interact with one another to affect teaching and learning. Zullig et al. (2010) indicated that school climate can affect students' academic achievement and success in addition to positive social and emotional development efforts. However, as pointed out by Cohen and colleagues (2009), these are not reflected in current educational policy or teaching practices (p. 149).

The components that make up school climate are multifaceted, ranging from the quality of interactions among the people that are part of the climate to the quality of climate-controlling strategies implemented. It is clear that the school composition does not automatically determine school climate; hence, changes to the school composition without changes to the school climate do not assure quality changes at the school level.

Normally, new teachers are often left to depend on their own skills to succeed or fail—working in isolation within the confines of their classroom's walls. Teaching is one of the most isolated and loneliest careers. As indicated by Smith and Ingersoll (2004), perhaps not surprisingly, teaching has also traditionally been characterized as an occupation with high levels of attrition (i.e., loss of practitioners to other occupations), especially among beginners (p. 682). The "revolving door" epidemic among teachers' ranks has had a profound effect on the quality of implementation of mentoring programs at the school level.

It was believed at one time that mentoring programs somehow provided a solution to the problem of teachers leaving the profession prematurely; but as indicated in this chapter, mentoring programs are no singular cure for teachers who come with extensive flaws. Smith and Ingersoll (2004) stated that teachers' induction is distinct from both preservice and in-service teacher training. "Preservice" refers to the training and preparation that candidates receive before employment. "In-service" makes reference to periodic upgrading, improvements, and additional training received on the job, during employment (2004, p. 683).

Fundamentally, induction or mentoring programs are not designed to provide more training requirements but are specifically created for teachers who are already on the job and have completed all requirements to commence employment. The mentoring programs are there to create a climate in which the new teacher with the assistance of a veteran acquires the skills to be able to connect theatrical knowledge to an understanding of real-world teaching. As stated by Smith and Ingersoll (2004), these programs are often conceived as a bridge, enabling the "student of teaching" to become a "teacher of students." As we already learned, mentoring programs range from a single orientation meeting at the beginning of the school year to a detailed and extensive program in which a series of activities and interactions will take place over a longer period of time.

In contrast, stories that portray help for new teachers are less well known in fiction or otherwise—for several reasons. One cause could be that little systematic knowledge exists about what can help new teachers. Another reason could be that, while the problems are universal, the solutions are individual and difficult to generalize (Meister, 1992, p. 6). According to Smith and Ingersoll (2004), mentoring programs themselves differ along the same dimensions, such as the following: (1) whether they include training for the mentors; (2) how much attention they devote to the match between mentor and mentee; (3) the degree to which mentors are compensated for their efforts, either with salary supplement or a reduction in other duties; and (4) whether an effort is made to provide mentors who have experience in teaching the same subjects and grade levels as their mentees (p. 683). Therefore, the mission of helping new teachers requires sustained and gradual effort to achieve subtle, but substantial, changes.

Notwithstanding the general consensus that mentoring programs are an important part of new teachers' development, not all school districts have implemented formal mentoring programs in their schools. Meister (1992) concluded that policy statements alone do not guarantee good programs, but they do often increase the likelihood that official notice will be taken of new teachers and that staff time, effort, and other resources will be assigned to them (p. 14).

New teachers often feel overwhelmed by the daunting task demanded by the classroom. Therefore, overly confusing and loosely planned mentoring programs will only lead to more anxiety and unnecessary stress, ultimately affecting the teachers' level of efficacy. The assistance provided by the mentoring program should be clear, incremental, and limited at any one time.

Thus, quality mentoring programs are supportive, long-term relationships between an experienced mentor and their less experienced mentees. The guiding idea of a mentoring program is to create an environment in which the mentor—or more experienced teacher—will pass on knowledge in the form of experiences that they have had during their long career. Mathur, Gehrke, and Kim (2012) indicated that effective teachers' decision making influences not only teacher practices in the classroom but also long-term choices about their remaining in the profession (p. 161). When teachers are able to conduct self-evaluation and can assess their own level of efficacy, they experience greater job satisfaction—which leads to better teaching and greater longevity.

Creating a positive school climate takes the work and commitment of the entire school community. As already stated, a poor school climate created by the managerial style of leadership can lead to a condition of distrust, chaos, and disrespect that hampers student and staff motivation, limiting their level of efficacy and student achievement. On the other hand, a climate created by an instructional leadership model leads to a climate in which a positive,

interactive, rich, supportive climate is seen as the base for a safe, respect-
ful, trustful, and motivational school environment. Principals who make the
transition to instructional leaders—and up their game to become climate controllers—thrive in the quest of creating an environment in which all of these
characteristics are able to function at the optimal level of efficacy.

SUMMARY

Although the research on mentoring talks about the benefits of mentoring
as an effective mechanism to provide teachers with support, we still see the
need for more work to be done in the areas of classroom application and
practice. Mathur et al. (2012) indicated that good mentoring programs have
been shown positively to influence beginning teachers' decisions to remain
in teaching. Furthermore, an emerging literature on mentoring outcomes also
has posed questions about the positive effects of quality mentoring relationships on the mentors in terms of the day-to-day decision making, classroom
practices, job satisfaction, enhancement of leadership skills, and improved
practice (2012, p. 155). Therefore, district and school leaders must continu-
ously evaluate their mentoring programs and process and concentrate on the
mentor-mentee quality of relationships to provide targeted support.

Climate controllers are not only deeply committed to instructional goals
but also solidly dedicated to creating and enhancing *professional communities* within the school. Blase and Blase (1999) indicated that leaders—who
move beyond instruction and develop structural conditions by providing
resources and support for the redesign of programs and apply the principles of
adult growth to staff mentoring programs and activities—are more successful
in improving teaching in their schools (p. 371). In addition, Blase and Blase
(1999) argued that these leaders develop core human and social resources; for
example, they promote the following: (1) positive school climate and group
development; (2) teamwork, collaboration, innovation, and continual growth;
(3) trust in staff and students; and (4) caring and respect to enhance teacher
efficacy.

Ganser (2002) indicated that principals should not forget that even the best
mentoring programs are only one part of the broader context of appropriate
and high-quality induction support for new teachers that enables them to
"come up to speed" more quickly than if they are organizationally abandoned
and are thus left alone to improve their work through "trial and error."

The current research on school climate does not give us a clear picture on
how to assess and improve school climate. However, it is evident that schools
do make a difference in what happens to the people who work and study in
that particular school environment. Kelley (1981) indicated that we know,

too, that focusing on any single climate dimension—such as *satisfaction*, or any particular audience, such as *teachers*—is a less-than-adequate approach to the design and implementation of school environments committed to the welfare of all participants (p. 183).

Ganser (2002) explained that with an effective and successful new teacher mentor program, everyone wins: the new teachers, veteran staff, the school community, and especially the children. By supporting mentoring programs in the ways described here, school principals can maximize the unquestionable value of new teacher mentoring as a central feature of the professional learning community that they lead (p. 11).

REFERENCES

Anderson, N. H. (1970). Averaging model applied to the size-weight illusion. *Perception & Psychophysics*, 8, 1–4.

Argyris, C. (1958). Some problems in conceptualizing organizational climate: A case study of a bank. *Administrative Science Quarterly*, 2, 501–20.

Black, G. L. (2010). Correlational analysis of servant leadership and school climate. *Catholic Education: A Journal of Inquiry and Practice 13* (4), 437–66.

Blase, J., & Blase, J. (1999). Principals' instructional leadership and teacher development: Teacher perspectives. *Educational Administration Quarterly 33* (3), 349–78.

Brookover, W. B., Schweitzer, J. H., Schneider, J. M., Beady, C. H., Flood, P. K., & Wisenbaker, J. M. (1978). Elementary school social climate and school achievement. *American Educational Research Journal 15* (2), 301–18.

Cohen, J., McCabe, E. M., Michelli, N. M., & Pickeral, T. (2009). School climate: Research, policy, practice, and teacher education. *Teachers College Record 111* (1), 180–213.

Cummings, G. (2011). Investing in teachers to invest in themselves. *Journal of Adult Education 40* (2), 19–23.

Daloz, L. A. (1999). *Mentor: Guiding the journey of adult learners. The Josey-Bass Higher and Adult Education Series.* San Francisco, CA: Jossey-Bass Publishers.

Feiman-Nemser, S. (1998). Teachers as teacher educators. *European Journal of Teacher Education*, 21, 63–74, doi: 10.1080/0261976980210107.

Feiman-Nemser, S. (2001). Helping novices learn to teach. Lessons from an exemplary support teacher. *Journal of Teacher Education*, 52, 17–30, doi: 10.1177/0022487101052001003.

Freiberg, H. J. (1998). Measuring school climate: Let me count the ways. *Educational Leadership 56* (1), 22–26.

Ganser, T. (2002). *Supporting new teacher mentor programs: Strategies for principals.* Office of Field Experiences, University of Wisconsin-Whitewater.

Green, K. (2006). No novice teacher left behind: Guiding novice teachers to improve decision-making through structured questioning. *Penn GSE Perspectives on Urban Education 4* (1), 1–9.

Gunbayi, I. (2007). School climate and teachers' perceptions on climate factors: Research into nine urban high schools. *Turkish Online Journal of Educational Technology 6*, 70–78.

Johnson, H. (2001). Administration and mentors: Keys in the success of beginning teachers. *Journal of Instructional Psychology 28*, 1–8.

Kelley, E. A. (1981). Auditing school climate. *Education Leadership 39*, 180–83.

Knowles, M. (1975). *Self-directed learning: A guide for learners and teachers*. New York, Cambridge: The Adult Company.

Lataille, M. L. (2005). Thoughts on teacher mentoring. *New England Mathematical Journal*, 60–63.

March, J. G. & Simon, H. A. (1958). *Organizations*. Oxford, England: Wiley.

Mathur, S. R., Gehrke, R., & Kim, S. H. (2012). Impact of a teacher mentorship program on mentors' and mentees' perceptions of classroom practice and the mentoring experience. *Assessment for Effective Intervention 38*, 154, 155–62.

Meister, G. R. (1992). Help for new teachers: Developmental practices that work. *Research for Better Schools, Inc.* Philadelphia, PA.

Moos, R. (1979). *Evaluating educational environments: Procedures, measures, findings and policy implications*. San Francisco: Jossey-Bass.

Newton, A. E. (1987). *Teacher quality: An issue brief*. Andover, MA: The Regional Laboratory for Educational Improvement of the Northeast and Islands.

Oreilly, R. (1975). Classroom climate and achievement in secondary school mathematics classes. Retrieved from http://files.eric.ed.gov/fulltext/ED101473.pdf .

Parker, M. A., Ndoye, A., & Imig, S. R. (2009). Keeping our teachers! Investigating mentoring practices to support and retain novice educators. *Mentoring and Tutoring: Partnership in Learning 17* (4), 329–41.

Perry, A. (1908). *The management of a city school*. New York: Macmillan.

Schwille, S. A. (2008). The professional practice of mentoring. *American Journal of Education 115* (1), 139–67.

Smith, T. M., & Ingersoll, R. M. (2004). What are the effects of induction and mentoring on beginning teacher turnover? *American Education Research Journal 41*, 681–714.

Tableman, B. (2004). *Best practice beliefs*. Lansing, MI: Michigan State University.

Tillman, L. C. (2005). Mentoring new teachers: Implications for leadership practice in an urban school. *Educational Administration Quarterly 41* (4), 609–29.

Zellers, D. F., Howard, V. M., & Barcic, M. A. (2008). Faculty mentoring programs reenvisioning rather than reinventing the wheel. *Review of Educational Research 78* (3), 552–88.

Zullig, K. J., Koopman, T. M., Patton, J. M., & Ubbes, V. A. (2010). School climate: Historical review, instrument development, and school assessment. *Journal of Psychoeducational Assessment 28*, 139–52.

Chapter 4

The Key Components of Mentoring in School Leadership

Preparation Programs and Leadership Assignments

Tyrone Bynoe

INTRODUCTION

Today's school administrators—whether at the district level or the building site—face unprecedented demands to perform effectively. Curricular uniformity through the emergence of the Common Core standards has required an increasingly diverse population to meet these standardized academic expectations.

This effort is an especially daunting responsibility for school managers confronting the double task of empowering lower-performing students while also meeting the unique needs of gifted and talented students. A school leader's imperative to prepare students for college and career readiness—while closing the learning gap—can appear impossible in the face of ongoing budgetary pressures, poor teacher quality, chronic low-performing schools, conflicting environmental pressures, and receded parental participation.

The recent high turnover of school leaders caused by the retirement of "baby boomers" only to be replaced with fewer "late bloomers" has created a leadership gap that is a challenge to fill. This problem is even further exacerbated when a state, such as Kentucky, has removed school funding from its principal internship program (HB235 14RS) and has shifted the burden to prepare first-year principals to school districts or affiliated higher education institutions.

Against this backdrop of formidable challenges and depleted support, recurring research findings affirm that the training, placement, and retention of successful school leaders will demand the vital support components of mentoring in school leadership preparation programs and within various school administrative assignments. To solve the leadership and support concerns addressed in the above research problem, I ask the following research questions:

1. What are the proven characteristics that typify effective mentoring in school leadership preparation programs for building principal licensure and the licensure of other school leaders?
2. What are the proven characteristics of mentoring that contribute to the development of expected knowledge, skills, and dispositions in school leadership licensure programs?
3. What are the proven characteristics that typify mentoring in on-site job settings regarding school principals and other school leaders?

OVERVIEW

This chapter reviews pertinent research literature to develop a conceptual model of effective mentoring in school leadership programs and in school leadership assignments. The conceptual approach of this chapter necessitates an initial definition of mentoring. This definition will be expanded by analyzing how school leadership preparation programs actually use effective mentoring and how local school communities incorporate effective mentoring into the lives of their school leaders.

DEFINITION OF MENTORING

Consensus in defining the term *mentor* is difficult since perspectives vary significantly on what role mentors fill—and what mentors do. Legends may be a good place to begin. In her dissertation, Doherty explains how the term *mentor* was derived from Greek folklore.

The story of Mentor is told in Homer's *Odyssey*. When Odysseus set off for the Trojan Wars, he instructed his wise advisor, Mentor, to stay and take charge of his son, Telemachus, serving as his counselor and advisor. Greek mythology also tells of Athene, the female goddess of wisdom, and how she would sometimes assume the form of Mentor. Conceivably, the other characteristics could also be added to Mentor, those of the mother figure and the wisdom of Athene (Doherty, 1999, p. 8).

Drawing from ancient western mythology, then, the term *mentor* refers to a wise person who is entrusted with the advisory responsibility of another. Within school leadership programs, mentors are experienced school leaders who advise newly employed or aspiring supervisors. This means that mentors impart their knowledge to protégés as trusted advisors.

A second distinct characteristic that defines mentors of school leaders in their programs is the mentors' impartiality. The act of mentoring is assumed to be impartial by experienced school leaders who have no formal evaluative role as supervisors of their administrative protégés or aspiring protégés.

Mentors interact with their protégés, who are aspiring school leaders, through both clinical-based courses embedded with field experience as well as within internship programs. Mentors also interact with first-to-third-year administrators as a protégé through advisory programs for newly appointed school leaders. In sum, the mentor in a school leadership context is an advisor-sage and an unofficial cooperator in relationship to his or her protégé. Figure 4.1 below depicts this foundational concept of mentoring as defined by its two basic components.

Research Question 1: *What are the proven characteristics that typify effective mentoring in school leadership preparation programs for building principal licensure and other school leaders?* Research affirms that high expectations and structure are among some of the most important characteristics of an effective mentoring program for school leaders. The literature that advocates for high expectations insists that an effective mentoring program must clearly delineate precise learning outcomes for protégés and aspiring school administrators (Gray, Bottoms, & O'Neill, pp. 22–23; Bush & Chew, 1999, p. 46).

In fact, these advocates disparage the idea that mentoring should typify a mere peer program that enables the aspiring school leader to identify with the experienced school leader to the point of making the new school leader comfortable with his or her assumed duties. Instead, this perspective maintains that seasoned leaders must train school leaders in specific competencies so that mentees are immediately ready to take school leader positions to tackle the formidable demands that accompany today's supervisory assignments.

The structure of mentoring programs is equally important. The United Kingdom's mentoring program for aspiring head teachers from the Education

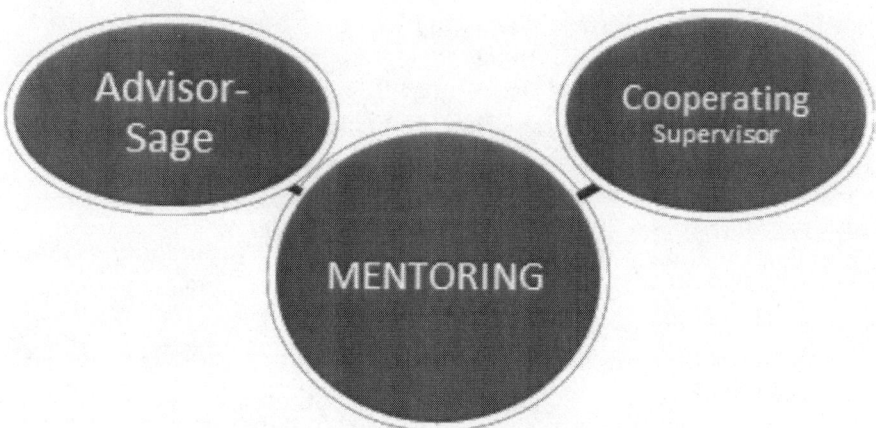

Figure 4.1   Components of Mentoring.

Reform Act of 1988 until 1996 is illustrative of this point. To become a head teacher during this period, a supervisory candidate had merely to participate on a voluntary basis in a peer-mentoring program through an internship that consisted of several sessions between the mentor and mentee (or protégé) from which the mentor would provide a form of peer support. While the local education authority's administrator coordinated these meetings to some degree, the mentee—and not the mentor—made arrangements of meetings and determined the nature of discussions during peer sessions.

By 1997, this process of legitimizing aspiring head teachers was supplanted with a training curriculum that culminated in a certification assessment for licensure. While the practice of peer mentoring coexisted with the new licensure program, it did not become part of this certification progress at this time due to having a structural inadequacy of preparation (Bush & Chew, 1999, p. 47).

Conversely, Singapore instituted a mentoring program in a British-adopted public school system that had a defined structure, since its Ministry of Education selected mentors who were rated as highly effective in their respective schools and among their professional peers. Singapore's head teacher's (principal's) mentoring program also provided a structured training course for aspiring head teachers, featuring specific competencies, codelivered programming, and constant evaluation (Bush & Chew, 1999, pp. 45–50).

Another element regarding the structure of a mentor-protégé relationship is that the mentor is committed to the protégé for a long period of time, such as over several semesters in a cohort program that uses a continuum of instruction in coursework culminating in a capstone project or during any of the first three years in a new building administrator's assignment. This extent of commitment distinguishes a mentor from a "coach"—a confidant to a new building administrator for a shorter period of time "involving conversations that support job-embedded learning" (Ontario Leadership Strategy, 2011, p. 10).

In fact, coaching typifies a learning relationship featuring a supervisor who imparts knowledge, skills, and dispositions to improve student learning. In contrast, mentoring in school leadership programs includes not only coaching but also the broader imparting of the entire skill set of effective school leadership for protégés making a career transition from pedagogy to school administration (Rhodes, 2012, pp. 246–48).

Several qualities regarding the structure of Singapore's mentoring program are important to reiterate and elaborate. Current research findings suggest that effective mentoring programs must contain a structure that is codesigned and codelivered by a university center in collaboration with a local school district community. Proponents of codesigned and codelivered mentor programs maintain that schools provide both a *contextual* and an *experiential* relevance that sole-authored university leadership programs usually lack.

These advocates argue that mentoring is an important piece in transforming the university's school leadership preparation programs into relevant clinical courses of study in the same way that assigning an aspiring physician to do a residency with a cooperating physician to learn his or her practice in medicine is a critical component in a doctor's training. This approach also stresses the need for university programs to recruit clinical faculty as mentors who are capable of equipping aspiring school leaders to apply insights garnered from education coursework to improve students' achievement and to thus transform school culture.

The National Council for Accreditation of Teacher Education (NCATE) articulates the expectation for university faculty in education preparation programs to recruit school-based faculty in its five standards on *Faculty Qualifications, Performance, and Development.* In its substandard 5D titled *Modeling Best Professional Practices in Service,* NCATE explains the target expectation of how educator preparation programs must be codesigned and codelivered with direct application to the imperative of university faculty assuming collaborative responsibility with its PK–12 constituents. They should try to recruit school-based faculty, and it authored: "All professional education faculty are actively engaged in dialogues about the design and delivery of instructional programs (mentoring) in both professional education and P–12 schools" (NCATE Professional Standards, 2008, p. 40).

A pertinent set of learning society standards, namely the Educational Leadership Constituent Council (ELCC) standards, emphasizes in Standard 7 that higher education institutions must recruit a qualified *on-site mentor* to provide embedded field experiences in courses and in an internship of a school leader preparation program. The substandard 7.3 stresses this requirement when describing a mentor: "Qualified On-Site Mentor" needed for on-site leadership.

These mentors should be able to show their experience as an educational principal "within a school and is selected collaboratively by the intern and program faculty with training by the supervising institution" (ELCC, 2011, p. 24). Since NCATE endorses ELCC standards as a set of professional expectations for certifying school leadership programs, this detailed expectation on the role of the on-site mentor is a very important requirement for school leadership programs to meet.

Another important component that research findings emphasize is that the structure of effective mentoring programs must contain embedded real-life field experience in coursework and throughout the internship, thereby imparting problem-solving skills that the aspiring school administrator must obtain. These field experiences not only contain mere direct observations but also participatory observations as well as implementation of applied competencies taught during in-class settings. A Southern Regional Education Board publication emphasized the vital role of mentors being used to structure prerequisite competencies and pertinent field experiences, and the Board found the following:

> Good mentors provide the day-to-day feedback . . . that will help interns transition from the role of classroom teacher (or other roles) to that of school leader. They know how to structure opportunities for interns to solve a range of school problems, first through observing and participating and then by actually leading teams in identifying, implementing and evaluating improvement interventions. (Gray, Bottoms, & O'Neil, 2007, p. 11)

Along with problems of not articulating the pertinent competencies for mentoring and the inability to structure potent mentoring programs, inadequate mentoring is rooted in the inappropriate selection of mentors. Too often, protégés (or mentees) identify their own mentors in localized and convenient school settings to monitor their field experiences in courses or to supervise internships and practicums within their local school settings. Unfortunately, these protégés are not always up to this task since, by definition, they lack severely the knowledge, skills, and dispositions to identify suitable mentors who will train, nurture, and help them mature in their schools' leadership preparation and licensure programs.

To correct this problem, the administration of university leadership preparation programs must first collaborate with the candidate to select his or her mentor. This explains why ELCC substandard 7.3 stresses the imperative that an intern cannot select his or her on-site mentor alone, but must do so in consultation with his or her supervising institution (ELCC, 2011, p. 24).

Second, university administrators must align their efforts with local school districts to identify appropriate clinical faculty as mentors as part of codesigning and codelivering the leadership program. In this way, the educator preparation program becomes an authentic service of instructional delivery, effectively combining theory with practice. By selecting mentors in this manner, school systems are able to provide increasing levels of resources and support, especially if university programs have memoranda of understanding from local communities to provide such support.

This strategic partnership between the local schools and university educator preparation programs become critically important when university budget reductions often compel these programs to eliminate vital components of clinical mentoring services.

Additionally, a faulty assumption on the part of university administrators concluded that school principals or administrators will automatically become effective mentors for the diverse and swelling number of emerging school leader candidates. Some effective administrators lack the prerequisite knowledge, skills, and dispositions to mentor aspiring leadership candidates.

In fact, in some cases school administrators who are effective at their jobs are not always able to communicate and transfer their own abilities to aspiring leadership candidates. Moreover, the pool of experienced, near-retirement-age administrators—who are largely white males in many communities—is sociologically different from the emerging pool of aspiring candidates, who are largely women and minorities in many university educator preparation programs. This sociological mismatch redramatizes a recurring problem that has been well documented by educational historians (Tyack & Hansot, 1982, pp. 232–33) and other educational researchers (Pavan, 1986, pp. 12–17). An Educational Alliance publication emphasized this faulty assumption and cultural disparity regarding the selection of mentors.

Robert Malone (2002), a research analyst with the Educational Resources Information Center (ERIC), cautions that artificially constructed mentor-protégé relationships can sometimes neutralize the effect of mentoring. "Even the most accomplished mentors," he writes, "can fail to connect with a protégé, resulting in a neutral effect relationship at best." Malone also points out that race and gender issues complicate the formation of mentor-protégé relationships.

The majority of school superintendents and principals who might serve as mentors are white males; yet more than 73 percent of all teachers who might aspire to the principalship are female. Generally, female and minority aspiring principals "cannot rely on traditional avenues for forming such relationships," writes Malone, suggesting the need for particular attention to mentor-protégé relationships for these groups (The Education Alliance, 2003, p. 13).

To recapture the research-based characteristics that typify effective mentoring in school leadership programs for aspiring school principals, Figure 4.2 can be further developed as shown below in Figure 4.3.

Research Question 2: *What are the proven characteristics of mentoring that contribute to the development of expected knowledge, skills, and dispositions in school leadership licensure programs?* An administrator must first possess the knowledge, skills, and dispositions of being an effective school leading practitioner in order to pass on his or her success to mentees. Equally important, the validation for an experienced supervisory practitioner to become a mentor must not be self-initiated or protégé-initiated. As explained in the previous section, the supervisor's school district must take the initiative to qualify this administrator and undertake the process of legitimizing him or her as a suitable mentor.

With this procedure clarified, the protégé should not be assigned to newly hired building administrators or to administrators who have been in the position for just one to three years. Only experienced administrators of four or more years in most cases are likely to possess the qualities needed to become

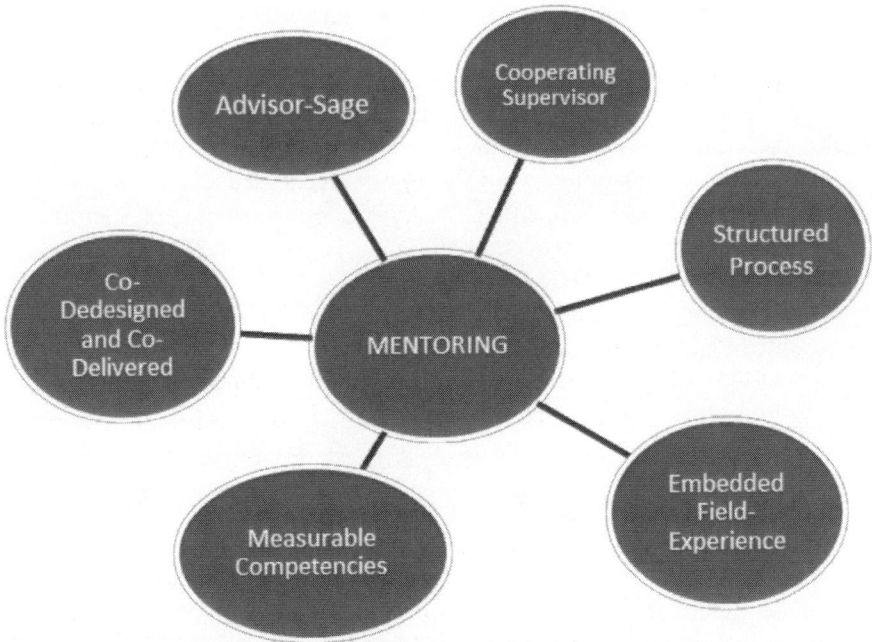

Figure 4.2   Key Qualities of Mentoring.

effective clinical faculty members of an educator leadership preparation program—and to certify as mentors of aspiring building administrators in this
program.

Against the baseline understanding of who may qualify to become a mentor to protégé in school leadership programs, it is now appropriate to identify
the specific knowledge, skills, and dispositions supervisory practitioners must
have to qualify as effective mentors in leadership preparation programs.

Knowledge

Along with exemplary competency as a school leader, the mentor must
understand the scope of supervision for the duties that he or she is monitoring
for the aspiring school leader. Ideally, mentors should be practitioners in the
same craft. School principal practitioners should not be mentoring aspirants
to the position of director of special education or districtwide curriculum
specialist. Despite there being consistent practices within the principalship
itself, it is advantageous that a mentor understand the precise scope of experience concerning the position that the aspiring administrator is training to
assume.

Hence, mentors who know the scope of the secondary school principal-ship—and are secondary school principals themselves—tend to qualify more as a mentor for protégé seeking the secondary school principalship than do mentors who understand the scope of—and are—elementary school principals. NCATE Standard 5A on *Qualified Faculty* stresses the need for mentors to know the scope experience of the position that they advise when this expectation states the following: "Clinical faculty (higher education and school faculty [i.e., mentors]) are licensed in the fields that they teach or supervise and are master teachers or *well recognized for their competence in their field*" (NCATE Standards, 2008, p. 38).

Mentors must have the insight that they are providing an *investment* of expertise as well as embarking on a *shared journey* with the protégé. The mentor's investment reinforces the fact that mentors provide meaningful and intentionally designed professional development to the long-term career maturation of his or her mentees. Concurrently, mentors embark on a shared journey with mentees to exchange sets of meaningful learning experiences where the outcome is of mutual benefit to some degree (Fletcher & Mullen, 2012, p. 7).

Skills

The skills that mentors must possess are in instructional consultation, com-munication, time management, reflective thinking, risk taking, role-playing, and simulation. Mentors must also have the skills to give impartial instruc-tional support and consultation. Mentors are not mere peer administrators but are specialized consultants who can provide the precise instructional support enabling protégés to mature in the aspects of instructional leadership, featur-ing—but not limited to—instructional programming, teacher supervision, and continuous assessment.

Mentors of aspiring school leaders must model effective communication. Since interpersonal skills constitute a key competency of administrative prac-tice, mentors must be able to model effective communication in listening, speaking, writing, and reading. Mentors must especially be able to guide pro-tégés in communication within the context of constantly changing drama and in spontaneously responding to multiple constituents. Through this guidance of imparting communication skills, mentors must particularly assist protégés in developing listening skills to instill fundamental competencies in process-ing, analyzing, and meeting multiple demands that various school constitu-ents often make simultaneously and with immediate response expectations.

Additionally, mentors must guide administrators to develop intuition alongside analytical skills so that aspiring administrators have the ability to conduct an environmental scan of external threats and opportunities to the local school as well as an internal audit of the school's strengths and weakness. Such skills help equip protégés in the art of strategic planning—decision making that will enable protégés to supervise the school while capitalizing, using, and building upon on the school's successes.

Guidance in developing listening leads to another important skill that mentors of aspiring school leaders must help these candidates develop—this is reflective thinking. Mentors must guide protégés to think and to rethink reflectively to develop problem-solving skills. They should be capable of the kind of deliberative contemplation that unpacks the complexities of problems to formulate cause-and-effect solutions. When using refined listening skills, mentors must also guide protégés to conduct direct observations of other employed school leaders through shadowing and effective data collection (Daresh, 2001, p. 52).

Finally, mentors must exhibit skills in role-playing and simulation to expose protégés to recurring and real-life administrative scenarios and to model and develop skills in formulating problem-solving responses during encounters with these scenarios. This is particularly true for newly employed administrators. Leadership preparation programs cannot prepare newly employed administrators for every situation and challenge in an administrative assignment. Mentors, then, are critical assets to new administrators in guiding these leaders through an effective transition and in developing the prerequisite skill set to perform effectively and to problem solve reflectively in their assignments (Mitgang, 2012, p. 24).

Dispositions

The dispositions that mentors of protégés in school leadership programs must exhibit consist of commitment, craftsmanship, ethical behavior, and collaboration. Again, a mentor is unlike a coach by virtue of the mentor's long-term commitment to the protégé's success. Therefore, mentoring assignments in sound administrative programs reveal that such principal preparation programs are not merely diploma or certificate mills for candidates to meet continuous teaching licensing requirements of the respective state accrediting agencies with no sincere sense of calling to this supervisory vocation.

Second, effective mentors will exhibit the disposition of being a master craftsman that trains aspiring leaders to become master artisans (Hall, 2008, p. 449). Since today's newly hired building administrator needs an entirely new skill set to build capacity in his or her school when responding to top-down accountability standards, such as the Common Core, newly recruited principals must receive embedded on-the-job training under the auspices of a master principal to learn the demands on the job. Mentors guide aspiring candidates in initial preparatory programs, but initial A Certification does not fully certify a candidate with the leadership readiness that is required in today's school leadership positions (DuBois, 2012, p. 1).

Third, effective mentors will guide protégés, motivated by the highest level of ethical behavior. Effective mentors will be impartial observers, especially for new administrators in administrative assignments. These valuable mentors will also become *critical friends* to the protégés, and provide honest feedback regarding the strengths and weaknesses of their protégés' development.

However, research reveals that mentors who are embroiled in the school politics of their local districts cannot be impartial in providing constructive feedback to their protégés. Rather than insulate newly employed administrators from the backlash of partisan reprisals and bickering, these so-called mentors often become the agent through which a newly employed administrator could be negatively evaluated.

Moreover, mentors who are overextended in meeting various school demands cannot provide the focused guidance and prerequisite time in training school leader candidates. This is particularly true for mentors who are exceptional administrators, and this shortcoming emphasizes the salient finding that an effective administrator does not automatically qualify to become an effective mentor of school leaders.

Another important disposition that effective mentors have is transforming the school from employing educators that advocate for independent problem solving to fostering a collaborative culture of interdependent problem solving (Ontario Leadership Strategy, 2011, p. 9). The field of school administration typifies leaders who are employed to be individual problem solvers, assuming all accountability of the school's success upon his or her shoulders.

While administrative regulation in most states acknowledges the building principal as the school's certified instructional leader, this does not suggest that the school administrator is to alone formulate problem-solving solutions for his or her school or be solely accountable for the school's success. Daresh (2001) acknowledges this fundamental and recurring problem in school administrative practice, and maintains that effective mentors will instill a collaborative and interdependent culture of effective supervision when he wrote:

> There is also a corresponding part of the world of school administrators in many school systems that proclaims, "You're the boss. Fix your own problems, and don't ask for help from anyone. If you can't do the job on your own, you're a failure." Indeed, the image of the leader as the Lone Ranger is very much alive in the world of school administration. . . . (p. 23)

Instead, asking for help when it is needed is an example of strength, not weakness. There is nothing wrong with having a system where the norm is for leaders to help other leaders. These assumptions are made because of another core belief: School administrators are important people who do important jobs, and as a result, all of the different forms of help that can be made available to these key school actors should be promoted (Daresh, 2001, p. 2).

This collaborative culture occurs not only among administrators within public schools, but also between mentors and university faculty who reinforce the nature of how mentors are instituted, structured, and organized. NCATE's substandard 5D on *Modeling Best Professional Practice in Service* articulates the target expectation in this manner: "(Professional faculty) collaborate regularly and systematically with P–12 practitioners (mentors) . . . They are actively engaged in a community of learners" (NCATE Standards, 2008, p. 40).

When reflecting on the section of this chapter on the knowledge, skills, and dispositions mentors must exhibit in school leadership programs, these competencies regarding mentors of aspiring school leaders are depicted on the next page in Figure 4.3.

The knowledge, skills, and dispositions of Figure 4.3 clarify the model conveyed in Figure 4.2, and further refines this model, which is illustrated below in Figure 4.4.

Research Question 3: *What are the proven characteristics that typify mentoring in on-site job settings regarding school principals and other school leaders?* While seemingly innumerable school leadership preparation programs have a form of mentoring, several selected programs epitomize

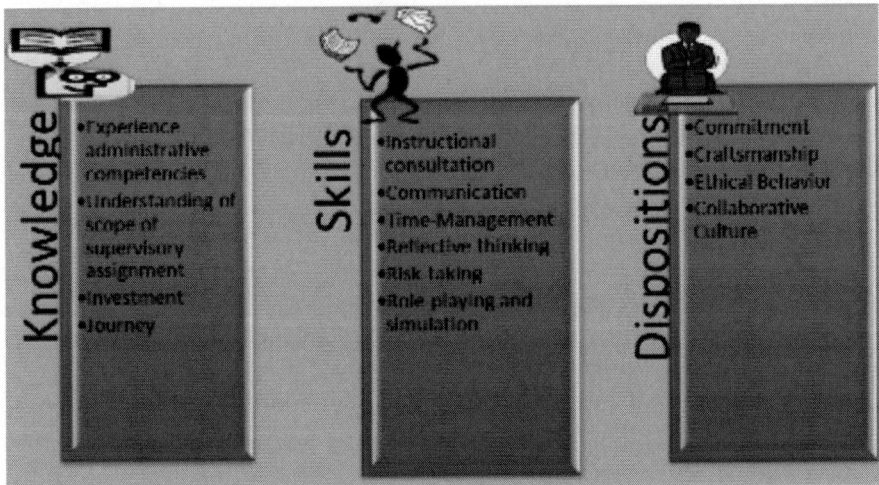

Knowledge
- Experience administrative competencies
- Understanding of scope of supervisory assignment
- Investment
- Journey

Skills
- Instructional consultation
- Communication
- Time-Management
- Reflective thinking
- Risk taking
- Role playing and simulation

Dispositions
- Commitment
- Craftsmanship
- Ethical Behavior
- Collaborative Culture

Figure 4.3   Knowledge, Skills, and Dispositions Needed for Mentors and Mentoring Practices of School Leadership Licensure Programs.

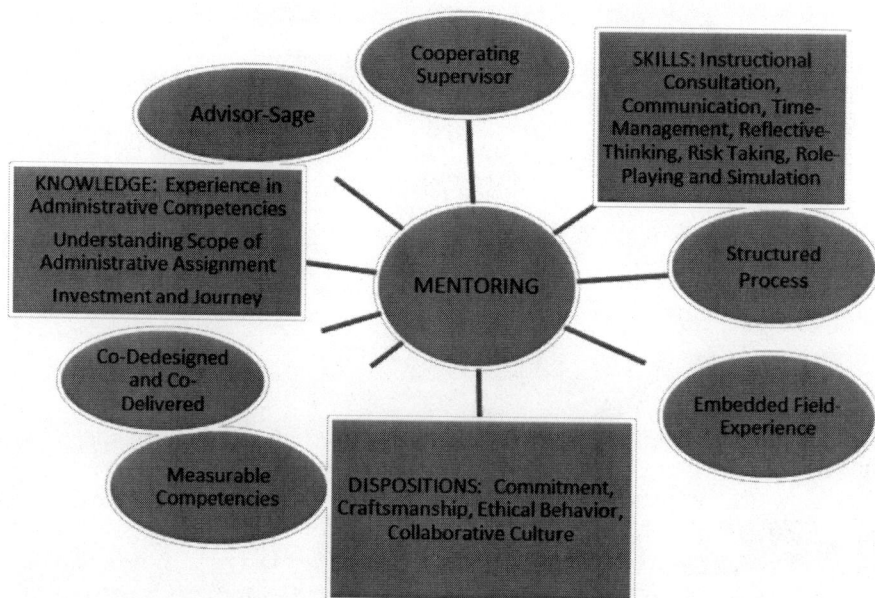

Figure 4.4   A Full Conceptualization of Mentoring in School Leadership Programs.

the components of the mentoring model described in Figure 4.4. All of these mentoring programs are codesigned and codelivered; they all also exhibit the essential collaborative aspect between the mentoring agencies and public schools. Many of these mentoring programs are separate entities that serve their protégés' affiliated school districts, and they can provide useful learning experiences for university preparation programs in school leadership. Perhaps the New York City Leadership Academy (NYCLA) serves as one of the country's largest mentoring programs for aspiring and new school leaders.

Developed in 2003, the NYCLA instituted an induction program to multiply the development of highly trained school leaders to help reform the metropolitan area's chronically failing schools. The specific challenge that NYCLA had faced in 2003 was that the mean student achievement of NYC's low-performing public schools had significantly lagged behind the average student achievement of schools in the rest of the state (Bynoe, Dissertation, 2004, p. 93).

One unique component of the NYCLA is its emphasis on both mentoring and coaching. The NYCLA's mentoring program includes a refined component of instructional coaching—a clear *structured process* that all mentoring programs should emulate. This structure of mentoring services includes signature competency-based coaching, online coaching mastery, local on-site coaching shadowing, and NYC-based coach shadowing. This mentoring/ coaching program requires its aspiring leadership candidates to master *measurable objectives* that promote high levels of student achievement. And this program requires extensive *embedded field experience* so that all candidates mature in expected and measurable leadership competencies (NYCLA, School Leadership Coaching Programs, 2003, p. 1).

The NYCLA's mentoring/coaching program has become such a flagship that it has been replicated in twenty-five states and in two other countries (NYCLA, How We Partner with Clients Across the Country, p. 1).

Local Mentoring Programs

In addition to NYCLA's mentoring/coaching programs, New York City area schools contain a number of effective mentoring programs that mirror several components of the mentoring modeled in Figure 4.3. One such program is Leaders in Education Apprenticeship Program (LEAP). Through a collaborative effort between the NYCLA and New York City Department of Education, LEAP provides a one-year mentoring program for aspiring leaders, and characterizes the mentor as *a master craftsman (or craftswoman)*.

One way LEAP mentors its apprentice-protégés is through the Sustainable Residency Project that calls for a one-year action plan resulting in documented and sustainable change in response to a concern articulated in the aspiring leader's school improvement plan. Mentors give as much as two-fifths of their work schedule to guide aspiring candidates to develop this aforementioned improvement plan in the Sustainable Residency Project (NYC Department of Education, LEAP).

Principal mentors in Prince George's County Public Schools in Maryland reinforce the imperative for mentors to meet one crucial *knowledge* expectation in Figure 4.3: to have substantial administrative *experiences and competencies* to qualify as a mentor. The district's job description for a principal mentor specifies a mentor's expected competencies, duties, and compensation.

Qualifications include—but are not limited to—instructional programming, data-driven instruction, communication and interpersonal skills, productivity software competency, professional development familiarity, and a minimum of four years of administrative experience (Prince George's County Public Schools, Compensation and Classification: Position Description). Along with these qualifications, the description of mentoring duties reinforces other important *knowledge* expectations, namely, that mentors understand *the scope of the administrative assignment* as well as the *journey* of the position that mentors must possess as shown in Figure 4.3.

State School Mentoring Programs

Delaware's Educational Leader Mentoring Program (ELMP) is an excellent example of a state school mentoring program for aspiring leaders. Established by the NYCLA, the ELMP provides a mentoring program that emphasizes how the *structure* of mentoring is authored in state regulation (Delaware Administrative Code 1503, 2014). ELMP assists the mentee in developing the disposition of *commitment* and the knowledge competency of *investment*. Newly hired administrators must participate in a three-year program of training, featuring the first year under the auspices of a trained mentor for sixty hours and for thirty hours during the second and third years.

Alabama's New Principal Mentoring (ANPM) program contains many of the roles, knowledge, skills, and dispositions of other school leader mentoring programs. It also has formidable requirements for its school leader mentors (Alabama Department of Education, 2011, p. 19).

One distinct feature of the ANPM program is that it requires all mentors to exhibit a refined code and *disposition of ethical behavior*. ANPM also requires a *commitment* for both the mentor and mentee of two years, and protégés must clock 72 hours per year or a total of 144 hours during the two-year mentoring period (Alabama Department of Education, 2011, pp. 18, 20).

One of Arizona's effective school leadership mentoring programs is under the leadership of the Rodel Foundation, which is a philanthropic organization with a vision to effectuate systemic success throughout Arizona's public school system. This mentoring program, known as Arizona's Rodel Exemplary Principal Initiative, contains exemplary principals from high-need, high-performing schools who are recruited through a rigorous selection process to become mentors.

In like manner, the Rodel Foundation recruits school leader candidates from high-need, high-performing schools through a competitive selection process to be placed with exemplary principals as mentors for two years. Mentors engage their protégés in the (Figure 4.3) skills of *reflective thinking*, *role-play*, and *simulation* (Rodel Foundation, 2014, p. 1).

School Leadership Mentoring in Professional Associations

Along with state and local mentoring programs, professional associations, such as the National Association of Elementary School Principals (NAESP), offer a formidable mentoring program for aspiring mentors and would-be elementary school principals. The training of mentors is especially important to note. Aspiring mentors must be experienced school administrators who complete the Leadership Immersion Institute (LII) as well as the Mentor-in-Training (MIT) program. And the LII is a three-day orientation to mentoring that emphasizes the expected principles of mentoring as well as NAESP's learning society standards: *What Principals Should Know and Be Able to Do.*

MIT is a nine-month program wherein a mentor is placed in an internship with a mentee, and both mentor and mentee must document aspects of the mentorship for seventy-two hours. During these contact hours, online discussions and monthly reflections based on the program's mentoring standards must be completed. Furthermore, mentors must offer support to peers through the online NAESP hotline as well as complete a culminating certification project (NAESP, 2014, National Principal Mentor Program).

All aforementioned tasks must be aligned to NAESP's School Leadership Mentor Standards, featuring mentoring competencies of high expectations, knowledge and skills, and instructional leadership; confidentiality and ethical behavior; clinical research and contribution; and collaborative culture promoting mentoring (NAESP, 2014, School Leadership Mentoring Competencies). Upon completion of the program, mentors are awarded a national certificate in mentoring and are recognized as mentors at the annual NAESP conference. In collaboration with higher education institutions, college credit can possibly be obtained when a mentor completes the MIT.

CONCLUSION

Mentoring for school quality in school leadership programs is defined through several key elements. The advisor-sage and cooperating administrator perform a role of close engagement with protégés in most mentoring programs in school leader preparation courses of study. Nevertheless, effective mentors do much more. Such leaders are involved in a structured process featuring measurable, codesigned competencies that are codelivered between program, clinical, and school-based faculty. This web of roles and attributes also are embedded in field experiences through the continuum of a candidate's leadership program and within the first three years of his or her placement as an employed administrative practitioner.

Mentoring with meaning for school leaders weaves prerequisite knowledge, skills, and dispositions through an active constellation of these roles and attributes. In a nutshell, effective mentors have knowledge through administrative experience, an understanding of these assignment's scope and duties, an investment of imparting professional expertise, and long-term insight into mentoring as a professional journey. Effective mentors possess refined skills as instructional consultants, communicators, reflective thinkers, risk takers, and simulators. Finally, effective mentors exhibit enduring dispositions of commitment, craftsmanship, ethical behavior, and collaboration.

The interplay of roles, attributes, knowledge, skills, and dispositions is quite evident in mentors representing local, state, and association school leader mentoring programs—and that are not necessarily university based. Therefore, university school leadership programs can learn quite a bit from school leader mentoring centers, such as the NYCLA's emphasis on its structured process, measurable competencies, and embedded field experience.

Much can be learned from LEAP's master craftsman contribution, Delaware's ELMP emphasis on how the structure and investment of mentoring is authored in state statutes, or Alabama's mentoring program requiring that mentors exhibit the highest form of human ethics. Moreover, university school leadership programs can benefit from the competencies that Rodel Foundation school principal mentors exhibit in terms of reflective thinking, role-play, and simulation. Finally, NAESP's rigorous training and internship competencies for school leader mentors will enable university school leader programs to improve on the prerequisite knowledge, skills, and dispositions for effective school leader mentoring.

Clearly, mentoring with meaning and school quality are an important and multifaceted training and responsibility that reinforces this profound fact: school leadership preparation programs certify candidates and practitioners in intricate learning processes and skill sets that are designed to supervise complex organizations and institutions of learning.

REFERENCES

Alabama Department of Education. (2011). Alabama new principal mentoring program guide. Birmingham, AL: Alabama Department of Education. http://alex.state.al.us/leadership/ANPM Program Guide.pdf.

Bush, T., & Chew, J. (1999). Developing human capital: Training and mentoring for principals. *Compare 29* (1), 41–52.

Bynoe, T. (2004). Adequacy and accountability: A study of resource sufficiency and the new learning standards in New York City high schools. Doctoral dissertation, Teachers College, Columbia University.

Compensation and Classification. (2014). *Principal in residence—NAESP mentor program: Position description.* Upper Marlboro, MD: Prince George's County Public Schools. http://www1.pgcps.org/compensationandclassification/index.aspx?id=190585.

Daresh, J. (2001). *Leaders helping leaders: A practical guide to administrative mentoring,* 2nd edition. Thousands Oaks, CA: Corwin Press, Inc.

Delaware Regulations. (2014). Administrative Code 1503. Educator Mentoring. http://regulations.delaware.gov/AdminCode/title14/1500/1503.shtml.

Doherty, T. (1999). The role of mentors in the development of school principals. Doctoral dissertation, Virginia Polytechnic University. http://scholar.lib.vt.edu/theses/available/etd-030799-163759/unrestricted/etd.pdf.

DuBois, L. (Summer 2012). *Principals' leadership and leadership principles: Creating professional development to help today's principals excel at leading teachers and schools.* Peabody Reflector. http://www.vanderbilt.edu/magazines/peabody-reflector/2012/07/principals-leadership-and-leadership-principles/.

Education Alliance: Brown University. (2003) *Making the case for principal mentoring. National Association of Elementary School Principals.* Providence, RI: Northeast and Islands Regional Laboratory. http://www.brown.edu/academics/education-alliance/sites/brown.edu.academics.education-alliance/files/publications/prncpalmntrg.pdf.

Educational Leadership Constituent Council. (2011). *Educational leadership program standards: 2011 ELCC building level.* Washington, DC: National Policy Board for Educational Administration. http://www.ncate.org/LinkClick.aspx?fileticket=zRZI73R0nOQ=&tabid=676.

Fletcher, S., & Mullen, C. (eds.) (2012). *The Sage handbook on mentoring and coaching in education.* Thousand Oaks, CA: Sage Publications.

Gray, C., Bottoms, G. & O'Neill, K. (2007). *Good principals aren't borne—they're mentored: Are we investing enough to get the school leaders we need?* Atlanta, GA: Southern Regional Education Board. http://www.wallacefoundation.org/knowledge-center/school-leadership/principal-training/Documents/Good-Principals-Arent-Born-Theyre-Mentored.pdf.

Hall, P. (February 2008). Building bridges: Strengthening the principal induction process through intentional mentoring. *Phi Delta Kappan 89* (6), 449–52.

Hazlett, D. (2008, September). Reflections on the principal mentor and mentee relationship. *The Pennsylvania Administrator—Educational Leadership*, 14–16. http://www.thiel.edu/assets/documents/academics/education/MentorandMenteeArticle.pdf.

Holloway, J. (April 2004). Mentoring new leaders. *Educational Leadership 61* (7), 87–88.

Kentucky Legislative Regulations. (2014). HB235 14RS. http://www.lrc.ky.gov/record/14RS/hb235.htm.

Malone, R. J. (2002). Principal mentoring: An update. *Research Roundup*, 18, 3–6.

Microsoft Partners in Learning. *Mentoring handbook for school leaders.* http://www.is-toolkit.com/knowledge_library/KL-MentoringHandbook.html.

Mitgang, L. (2012). *The making of the principal: Five lessons in leadership training.* New York: The Wallace Foundation. http://www.wallacefoundation.org/knowledge-center/school-leadership/effective-principal-leadership/Pages/The-Making-of-the-Principal-Five-Lessons-in-Leadership-Training.aspx.

NAESP. School leadership mentor competencies. Alexandria, VA: NAESP. http://www.naesp.org/sites/default/files/NAESP Mentor Competencies.pdf.

National Council for Accreditation of Teacher Education. (2008). *Professional standards for the accreditation of teacher preparation institutions.* Washington, DC: NCATE.

National Mentor Training and Certificate Program. (2014). *National principal mentor program.* Alexandria, VA: NAESP. http://www.naesp.org/mentor.

New York City Department of Education. *School leaders: Leaders in education apprentice program (LEAP) mentor principal.* http://schools.nyc.gov/AboutUs/

workinginNYCschools/leadershippathways/Opportunitie s/schoolleadership/Mentors+for+LEAP.htm.

New York City Leadership Academy. *How we partner with clients across the country.* Long Island City, New York: NYC Leadership Academy. http://www.nycleadershipacademy.org/how-we-partner-with-clients.

New York City Leadership Academy. *School leadership coaching programs: Development and improvement.* Long Island City, New York: NYC Leadership Academy. http://www.nycleadershipacademy.org/school-leadership-coaching-program.

O'Mahoney, G. (April 2003). Through their eyes: The changing role of the principal mentor as seen by beginning principals. *Management in Education 17* (2), 15–18. http://mie.sagepub.com/content/17/2/15.full.pdf+html.

Ontario Leadership Strategy. (2011). *Mentoring for newly appointed school leaders: Requirement manual.* Toronto, CA: Ontario Ministry of Education. http://www.edu.gov.on.ca/eng/policyfunding/leadership/pdfs/2011Mentoring.pdf.

Pavan, B. (April 1986). *Mentors and mentoring functions perceived as helpful to certified aspiring and incumbent female and male public school administrators.* Paper presented at the Annual Meeting of the American Education Research Association. San Francisco, CA. http://files.eric.ed.gov/fulltext/ED269884.pdf.

Rhodes, C. (2012). Mentoring and coaching for leadership development in schools. In *The Sage handbook on mentoring and coaching in education.* Edited by S. Fletcher & C. Mullen. Thousand Oaks, CA: Sage Publications.

Rodel Foundation. (2014). *Rodel exemplary principal initiative—Fact sheet.* Scottdale, AZ: Rodel Foundation. http://www.rodelaz.org/initiatives/principal-initiative/rodel-exemplary-principal-initiative-fact-sheet/.

Spiro, J., & Mattis, M. (March 2007). *Getting principal mentoring right: Lessons from the field.* New York: The Wallace Foundation. http://www.wallacefoundation.org/knowledge-center/school-leadership/principal-training/Documents/Getting-Principal-Mentoring-Right.pdf.

Tyack, D., & Hansot, E. (1982). *Managers of virtue.* New York: Basic Books.

Chapter 5

A Cultural Approach to Mentoring New Teachers

Donna Redman, Sharon Conley,
and Terrence E. Deal

The revolving door of beginning teachers has been a persistent problem in American education for many years. The cause is often attributed to the isolation of teachers in their private domains and the "sink or swim" attitude that prevails in many schools. New teachers typically receive little socialization to their new school, notoriously inherit the worst classroom assignments, and are then abandoned to fend on their own. As a result, they quit after one or two years.

Reformers in several states have concluded that the key problem is insufficient individual support at the school level and have created formal mentoring programs as a remedy. Nearly all of these state-sponsored programs are prescriptive, focused on the technical aspects of teaching, and in most cases they are tied closely to statewide teaching standards. Mentoring has now become the latest in a long series of educational reform initiatives—or buzzwords.

Acculturation, socialization, or onboarding of new members is a perennial problem for all human organizations. Newcomers need to learn how to carry out their puzzling new responsibilities but also master "the ropes"—the unique ways of their new tribe. If they are fortunate, a helpful person will appear to guide them through the odd labyrinth. Some newcomers even seize the initiative and seek an "old hand" as their compassionate guide.

We call these supportive people *mentors*. It's not a new concept. It has roots in Greek mythology. As the story goes, Odysseus placed his friend Mentor in charge of his son, Telemachus, as he left to fight in the Trojan War. Later, as only Greek mythology could depict, the goddess Athena visited Telemachus, disguised as Mentor. She became the source of sage but nebulous advice: "Telemachus, where your own intelligence fails, a god will inspire you. For I think the gods have blessed both your birth and your manhood" (Homer, 1945).

Notice that the goddess of wisdom's advice was neither specific nor directive. It left a lot to Telemachus's discretion. And thus is the magic of mentoring. The novice is not an empty vessel to be filled; novices also bring something to the relationship. Mentoring works best when the rookie's insights and previous experiences are recognized and valued—and even copied by others.

As time has passed, the term *mentor* has taken on many new meanings, most with fidelity to a core notion; that is, a helpful, wise person serving and guiding a wistful protégé. Some interpretations of Greek mythology cast the male, Mentor, as the practical side of the mentoring relationship, and the female, Athena, as the supportive or nurturing feature. Both are necessary for a successful mentoring experience (Colley, 2000).

Mentoring is a natural process. It can happen informally without either party ever acknowledging it officially. It can focus on work-related issues but widen its focus to personal matters. It is based on trust and confidence. It does not attempt to proselytize but rather to enlighten. Knowledge transmitted is very often tacit rather than explicit. Even when the parties disperse, lessons conveyed through the relationship persist in memory and often in use.

We suspect that, over the years, mentoring has undergone a shift from a person to a procedure; and it is rather informal to prescribed in many fields, especially in education. This raises several questions about current statewide efforts to improve teacher retention through mentoring programs:

1. What do new teachers (mentees) actually learn from mentors? Tacit knowledge? State standards?
2. Is what the novice brings in terms of new ideas recognized?
3. Is mentoring a choice between two people, or are mentors assigned?
4. Is mentoring still an age-old ritual between master and novice, or has it become a bureaucratic routine?
5. Is mentoring the real problem of new teacher exit, or is it a deeper issue of teacher acculturation?
6. Are the existing shortcomings of schools structural or cultural?

As most rationally based federal or state reform initiatives come upon the chaotic, capricious life in schools, the fit is almost always imperfect and "shambolic" (as a sham and symbolic). Ideas that sound and appear to be solid and efficacious on paper—or in rational policy circles—tend to shred and/or shrivel when exposed to the fragility, complexity, and humanity of school organizations. The history of school reform certainly bears this out (Deal & Redman, 2013). Here we look at California's Beginning Teacher Assessment Program (BTSA) as an example of a rational, technical approach to teacher retention. How is this reform actually playing out in schools? We then take a brief look at an acculturation effort in a top performing business and offer a cultural view of school shortcomings. Can education learn anything from these initiatives?

CONTEXT FOR THE BEGINNING TEACHER SUPPORT PROGRAM (BTSA)

BTSA is enmeshed in a broader interest in mentoring or induction programs in other sectors and other countries (Howe, 2006; Rhodes & Beneicke, 2002). During the 1980s, many school districts' mentoring programs sprang up around the country (Huling-Austin, 1990), but between 1990 and 2000, the proportion of new teachers involved nearly doubled. This is due, in part, to the widespread interest in mentoring across the board, in business (Kahle-Piasecki, 2011) as well as education.

Because schools are particularly vulnerable to "new ideas in good currency," many state legislatures seized upon mentoring as a new panacea for school improvement (Ingersoll & Strong, 2011). What had been a natural process in schools with positive robust cultures or high levels of teacher collaboration now became an official, programmed, and fixed effort on the part of state bureaucrats. In formulating policy, they neglected to consider evidence from an earlier study suggesting that teachers formally assigned to mentors often sought help elsewhere (Tellez, 1992). They also overlooked previous research documenting the supportive role of the principal, the contribution of a positive context or culture, and the impact of teacher collaboration or teaming in bolstering the beginning teacher's longevity.

ELEMENTS OF BTSA

At the heart of BTSA is the California Standards for the Teaching Profession (CSTP), six standards intended to guide teachers as they define and develop their practice. In BTSA, new teachers receive mentoring and ongoing support in their first two years of teaching, and mentors receive specific training (Howe, 2006). The program provides mentors with three days of initial state-approved training and various tools including assessment rubrics and state teaching standards (Feiman-Nemser & Carver, 2012; Norman & Feiman-Nemser, 2005). In addition, mentors are asked to attend monthly meetings and receive professional development in coaching and assessing. In many cases, mentors are relieved of part or all of their teaching duties and carry out their responsibilities full or part time, and are compensated with a stipend.

Mentees are also required to attend initial and monthly professional development seminars and workshops, focusing on such topics as classroom management, time management, and technology. In addition, they complete individualized induction plans to identify areas for professional growth (Pine, 2006).

In sum, BTSA has transformed a cultural process of acculturation or induction into a bureaucratic process focused primarily on the technical aspects of classroom teaching. The key question is: How is the program working?

EVIDENCE OF SUCCESS

Because of BTSA's scope and visibility, it has received considerable attention. In 1998, Mitchell, Scott, Hendrick, and Boyns conducted a large-scale evaluation of the program. Teachers' perceptions of the mentoring experience were generally positive, but they ranked it consistently lower than those of support providers (mentors) or administrators. The evaluators pointed out several tensions that needed to be resolved to assure the program's success:

- Meeting objective standards versus building close collegial relationships between beginning teachers and support providers
- Creating records versus focusing on support
- Standardizing program design versus maintaining local initiative
- Creating a context of induction support versus focusing on student learning
- Responding to new teacher needs versus moving them toward standards of professional practice
- Linking assessment with support in contexts typically providing neither
- Maintaining program quality versus expanding rapidly to serve all new teachers

In 2013, Koppich, Humphrey, Bland, Hennan, and colleagues reviewed BTSA in a broader context of all state policies affecting beginning teachers. The title of their report, "The Bumpy Path to a Profession," provides an inkling of their conclusions. The chief problem is the gnarly linkage among state policies regarding temporary credentials, BTSA, clear credentialing, evaluation of beginning teachers, and the tenure process.

Here we focus on the report's findings that relate to BTSA specifically. Many relate to the tensions forecast by the earlier (Mitchell et al., 1998) study.

Rookie teachers have a heavy load to bear. They are trying, in addition to personal tunings and adjustments, to navigate a strange new work situation, get their classrooms in order, and bring twenty or so unique young personalities into some sense of social order to master new subjects. Watching superhero Arnold Schwarzenegger's tortuous struggle with a kindergarten class in the classic film provides a vivid visual testimony of just how hard that can be.

New teachers interviewed by the study's authors often complained that the program designed to ease their way into the teaching profession was adding to their load. Two burdens stood out. First, the BTSA training and curriculum most often duplicated teacher preparation experiences. The added redundancy took time away from other more important teaching tasks without any apparent added value. While one-on-one time with mentors helps, plodding through "old stuff" hinders.

Second, the program's paperwork requirements are almost uniformly deemed burdensome, duplicative, and unrelated to induction. One support provider commented:

> Honestly I feel bad about all the paperwork. . . . Is it really helping them [beginning teachers] to be better teachers or is it just adding more stress? . . . Sometimes a lot of it feels redundant, over and over, kind of saying the same things.

Our 2014 interviews with both mentors and beginning teachers confirm these impressions. Amy Gregory served as a BTSA mentor for five years and shared her experience as a mentor.

> Before I was involved with BTSA, I understood the importance of having a school site mentor assigned to new teachers. I willingly took on the role as a mentor for new English teachers at my school and, especially, those in my grade level. My motive from this stemmed from my own experience as a new teacher. I remembered when I began teaching and that there was no one willing to help me with curriculum, materials, knowledge of the campus and staff, or programs at the school. I felt lost, scared, and alone. This experience helped me understand the importance of having a mentor available to a new person on campus, whether a new teacher, or one with experience who is new to the subject area or school.

When I began mentoring through BTSA, I found the new teachers were anxious for my help and valued the help with specifics of the campus and obtaining materials, as well as information about the curriculum of the grade-level subject. They were receptive to the classroom observations and suggestions made by the mentor to help with classroom management or instruction. It seems that most of the teachers were looking for tips of the trade on how to get through the day in a classroom.

But many of the benefits of these relationships were buried in the bureaucracy of the formalized process. Most of the paperwork and activities were time-consuming and not worthwhile. Also, the BTSA director in my district made it very difficult with her inflexibility and excessive requirements and rules. Time spent at meetings was not worthwhile, especially since they required time out of the classroom. The reports that needed to be turned in were a waste of time and an unreliable way of assessing the progress of the program implementation. The end-of-the-year ceremonies were not meaningful to everyone and should have been optional, and the notebook required of the mentee seemed punitive and of no use in the future. Although there were program standards that were driving the process, my role as a mentor was not influenced by them. I felt my part was to help the new teacher adjust to the job, gain expertise in classroom instruction and management, and work through concerns and questions about the job, the school, and the community.

In reflecting on the process as a whole and my role as a mentor, I believe the new teachers truly benefitted from bits and pieces of the program, mainly the relationships they fostered and the experiences they gained from their mentors. I enjoyed sharing any expertise I could and helping someone to have some positive experiences in a program that already carried so many negative feelings in its participants.

Scott Gordon is a novice teacher who recently completed his BTSA induction. His story illustrates the importance of the mentor relationship, and highlights the frustrations with some of the formalized program requirements:

> When I began induction, I was hoping to learn more strategies for being successful in my own classroom. I was thankful to have been paired with someone of experience who could realistically provide for me the "ins and outs" in the life of a teacher. My time spent with my coach was the most valuable and beneficial part of BTSA.

What frustrated me the most was the inordinate amount of paperwork I was required to complete and the amount of traveling I had to do to attend some of the required meetings. I gained much more from informal discussions with my coach than I did from filling out papers in a procedural process and driving to remote locations in order to complete the program requirements. If BTSA focused more on the relationships rather than the process, I think new teachers would find it extremely beneficial.

A more recent (2014) study focused specifically on the mentor-mentee relationship in a large sample of BTSA participants. There the program appears in a more favorable light. When we look at the mentor-mentee relationship, it fares well. The California Commission on Teacher Credentialing (CTC) recently reported the findings of a statewide survey of participating teachers (mentees) and support providers (mentors) (CTC, 2014).[1] The resulting sample was large—of approximately 15,500 participating teachers and

7,500 support providers—and had a response rate of over 80 percent for both groups (p. 3).

According to the participating teachers surveyed, BTSA support providers and the program's induction activities had a high impact in several areas. Examples of functions rated as effective are as follows (e.g., numbers indicate percentages of teachers rating BTSA support providers/professional development opportunities as having "moderate" or "strong" impact):

1. Develop[ing] my repertoire of teaching strategies (75.9)
2. Assessing student needs and differentiating instruction (including analysis of student work) (73.1)
3. Using results from assessment data to design instruction (68.7)
4. Using technology as a teaching tool (59.8)
5. Prioritizing the professional workload (57.9)

The survey also found that 71.4 percent of participating teachers reported meetings with mentors to be weekly or more often, with the majority (55 percent) reporting them to be weekly (p. 4). Further, over three-quarters of mentee respondents (80.1 percent) felt that they were "well matched" (p. 5) with their support providers. By and large, mentees also reported having observations by mentors in their classrooms. According to 37.5 percent of participating teachers, observations occurred more than three times during the current year; for another 58.1 percent, observations occurred two or three times over the year (p. 5). However, it was not clear from the report whether mentees also had an opportunity to observe their mentors teaching.

Other studies point out that the school context plays a decisive role in how well the mentoring relationship plays out. In schools with an existing high degree of collaboration among teachers, the BTSA-sponsored mentorship appears to work better than in schools where teachers operate independently in individual classrooms. BTSA also showed better results in higher, rather than lower, socioeconomic schools.

Research efforts to link BTSA mentoring to important outcomes such as teacher retention and student test scores have shown some positive effects, but Ingersoll and Strong (2011) caution us to be wary of drawing any conclusions until more controlled studies are completed.

A CULTURAL VIEW OF MENTORING

As one imaginatively muses, a driving metaphor guides most efforts to improve schools. It is revealed in the current language: *standards, outcomes, accountability,* and *formalization.* It is essentially the language of a manufacturing business or factory: a production line where young people receive information from a teacher and then are tested to see how well they have mastered it. Great care is taken to assure that all students are shaped by a common metric. Variations are channeled into other processes or labeled as defects and discarded. Stepping back, it appears to be the guiding image of schools shaping many mentoring programs.

There is another way to think about schools, artfully articulated by Willard W. Waller in 1932:

> Schools have a culture that is definitely their own. There are, in the school, complex rituals of personal relationships, a set of folkways, mores, and irrational sanctions, a moral code based on them. There are games, which are sublimated, wars, teams, and an elaborate set of ceremonies concerning them. There are traditions, and traditionalists waging their world-old battle against innovators. (1932, p. 96)

More recently, his view was reinforced by Nias, Southworth, and Yeomans (1989), who describe "cultures of collaboration" held together by the small details of school life that give it meaning and value:

> in the gestures, jokes, and glances that signal sympathy and understanding; in kind words and interest shown in hallways and outside classroom doors; in birthdays, treat days and other little ceremonies; in overt praise, recognition and gratitude; and in sharing and discussion of ideas and resources. Without the reciprocity that comes from such informal collaborative relationships, observe Bird and Little (1986), the whole purpose of [mentoring] is threatened. (Hargreaves & Dawe, 1990, p. 238)

The underlying images of schools and classrooms become that of a special culture or temple where more is going on than meets the rational eye. We all have memories of what it was, though it's hard to express. We remember teachers who made a difference in our lives, even though we often can't remember exactly what they taught. But we can vividly recollect who they were and how they made us feel. These deeper purposes lie at the heart of the teaching profession. Techniques, while important, are only part of the game: "Ends and means, purposes and practices are tightly bound together in the profoundly moral craft that teaching is" (Hargreaves and Dawe, 1990, p. 239).

This deeper aspect of teaching and its impact are extremely difficult to quantify or measure. As Albert Einstein once observed: "Some things are hard to count and many things that can be counted don't count."

Viewed through a *cultural* lens, mentoring is only part of the process of acculturation, the rites of passage that induct new members into the history, values, beliefs, language, and ways of a social group. New teachers need an intense formal orientation experience at the district and school levels followed by additional informal gatherings led by the informal priest or priestess and other informal cultural players. Following these larger occasions, grade level or team meetings ought to reinforce the cultural themes of who we are and how we do things in the school and classrooms. Then other teachers or teams can offer specific help or assistance, some eventually becoming potential mentors. But mentoring is embedded in a schoolwide process of inducting the newcomer into becoming a full-fledged member of the school's cultural fabric.

MARGARET AND JOAN: A MENTORING TALE

An illustration is provided by a composite story of a new teacher taking her first assignment at a low-income elementary school (Bolman & Deal, 1994).

Joan Hilliard is a typical new teacher—who just graduated from a teacher education program at a local university—reporting for her orientation at Pico Elementary School. Her expectations of what it will be like are jostled initially when she runs into the school custodian who gives her a few tips on teaching and student discipline. Her next encounter is with the school secretary who explains that the principal has been called to the district office and will be unable to keep his scheduled appointment with her. The secretary then gives Joan a school tour, and her knowledge and tone of command begins to give Joan the impression that she, rather than the principal, is really in charge of the school.

Later, Joan joins some of the older faculty at a local bar. They welcome her. They also help fill her in on her day's experiences and offer their take on how the school really works. They explain that the custodian is the community's eyes and ears on what goes on inside Pico and tell her not to be surprised if he listens at the door to her classroom to a lesson and gives her feedback shortly thereafter. The faculty reinforces her observation about Phyllis: she really does run the school. They regale her with stories, events of the past, and help her begin to understand some of the school's peculiar ways.

In days to come, she runs into Margaret Juhl, an older teacher, absent from the meeting at Jocko's, whom everyone seems to revere. Margaret's warm greeting and offer of support, if needed, make Joan feel she's found at least one person she can really count on.

As time passes, Margaret seems to show up out of nowhere to provide support:

Joan sat at her desk, her face buried in crossed arms. It had been the day from Hell. Her little nemesis, Roscoe, had been on a tear with Armando, his partner in making trouble. Together, they enlisted their classmates into their destructive frolic. Even Heidi, her top student, joined the bedlam. At the low point in her depressed soliloquy, she heard a familiar voice at her classroom door. "Tough day?"

Margaret came in and sat across from Joan. "We've all had them. My first years were horrific. I thought about quitting almost every day. I'm not sure why I stayed. I was stubborn, I guess, and didn't have anything better to do."

"But you're the best teacher at Pico," Joan protested.

"Not then. After a couple of years, the light bulb lit up: I wasn't teaching my kids. I was only thinking about the content I was trying to stuff into their heads. But I didn't know them. When I was studying to be a teacher, we learned lesson plans and teaching strategies, but we didn't think much about what kids need or the dynamics of a classroom. Do you know what really did help? I took a course at the University."

"It was about social organizations. I learned that schools are a lot like other organizations. Human dynamics rule the roost. Classrooms are the same—only in miniature. I started to rethink what it means to be a teacher. I'd been thinking of myself as a fount of knowledge, pouring content into empty minds. Content is part of the job, but I realized I also needed to be a classroom manager and leader."

"Classroom manager and leader" echoed in Joan's mind as she drove home.

Margaret was there again to provide sage advice about conflict following a particularly acrimonious faculty meeting. Margaret had verbally lashed out at the principal. He, in turn, fought back. The encounter upset Joan, who was not comfortable with such highly charged encounters:

"Joan, when I was younger I used to pussyfoot around conflict. As a little girl, I heard all the messages about being nice and not upsetting anyone. But I've learned since that you don't do any favors by holding back and keeping people in the dark."

"I heard those same messages," Joan said. "It's still hard for me to deal with all the tension and hurt feelings."

Margaret replied, "Me too, but teaching is not an exact science. We're not always going to agree with one another. When we're at odds with things that we care about, how in the world can we talk about disagreements without having anyone feel anything?"

Increasingly, over a year of working together, Joan realized she could call on her mentor for help when needed. Having gained Joan's trust that she will be supportive yet thought provoking, Margaret is able to share her perspective on most anything. When the latest new school improvement initiative—shared decision making—hit Pico, she got more chances. Teachers at the school were now required to become involved in schoolwide decisions, sharing authority with the principal. Joan was one of the first to volunteer, but things were not working out the way they were supposed to.

Joan sensed that she was rapidly losing her authority to be effective as chair of the discipline committee. The question was what she could do about it. She once again called on her trusted mentor.

"It's not just you," Margaret said reassuring, "the same thing is happening in lots of schools. Everyone's talking about empowering teachers and sharing decision making but the powers that be are also telling principals they are supposed to be strong and involved instructional leaders." "A couple of my old friends are principals—they went over to the dark side," said Margaret. "They often feel in a bind. They don't want to step on teachers' toes but they feel accountable."

"I think I see the problem," said Joan. "I agree, the principal is supposed to lead and a lot of the council members feel the same way. But as chair of the committee, I am supposed to be its leader. But the principal attends most all the meetings. People are confused about who's really in charge. I want to head the group but without usurping his authority."

"So it gets very baffling," said Margaret. "You're supposed to be chairing, but the principal is always there, undermining your say so. It's like a dance where no one's sure who's leading, who's following, and what rhythm you're supposed to be listening for. Some people are trying to waltz and others are doing hip-hop. Shared decision making is a good idea but it's tough to make it work."

Margaret also helps Joan when she becomes discouraged with standards, test scores, accountability, and the technical aspects of teaching. She helps her come to terms with more fundamental values of education and teaching: hope, faith, and belief.

"A classroom has to be a place of hope. It has to have meaning to build faith."

"What do you mean by faith?" asked Joan.

"Faith is believing in things when everyone tells you not to. It's believing in Roscoe even when his record tells you you're fooling yourself. It's convincing Roscoe to have confidence in himself, even though almost no one else ever has. It's getting his parents to have faith in him and what school can mean. Even more important, teachers have to believe in themselves and their work." Margaret explained: That's where I think we've fallen down. Just pick up any magazine or newspaper. Listen to the conversations in restaurants. Think about how we teachers talk when we're together. The public has lost confidence in us and we've lost faith in ourselves. Can we ask anyone to believe in what we do when we don't? No wonder they are asking for hard evidence."

Finally, after Margaret tragically passed away, Joan reflects on Margaret's lasting influence and presence. Coming full circle, now Joan becomes an informal mentor to a new teacher.

Two weeks after Margaret's funeral, Joan found herself sitting with a new teacher, Francesca King, on a carved wooden bench under the oak tree cast in the shadow on Pico's Margaret Juhl patio. It was a beautiful September day, and she asked if they could meet somewhere away from the classroom. Joan automatically suggested the patio. Whenever she went there she felt Margaret's presence.

As Francesca started to talk, it was clear she wanted a setting well away from the chaos that has reigned in her classroom that day. When Joan asked, "How's it going, Fran?" words tumbled out in an almost frantic stream.

"It's going downhill fast; my class is out of control. I don't know what to do about it, I'm afraid I'm in over my head. Maybe I should quit now before it gets any worse."

Joan smiled. "At about this point in my first year as a teacher I was ready to quit too."

MENTORING APPROACHES IN OTHER ORGANIZATIONS

Educators and those who make education policy are drawing the wrong lessons from top performing businesses. They assume such organizations succeed mainly because of clear standards, programmed activity, and measurable outcomes (much like the factory imagery discussed earlier). This, however, is not the primary driving force in their solid performance over time. Instead it is a culture, woven over time, consisting of values, rituals, ceremonies, and stories that assure success.

These prosperous businesses believe that culture comes first; profits follow. Accordingly, is vital that new members learn, understand, and share cultural norms, values, and ways. The socialization process is carefully planned and scripted. Mentoring is only one part of these intense goings-on. Experience has confirmed that time and effort devoted to initial "on-boarding" pays dividends in higher performance, greater satisfaction, stronger commitment, and longer tenure of new hires.

As an example, Ritz-Carlton Hotels are touted as among the best in providing superlative guest service. They have also been singled out as tops among other companies in the way they socialize new employees. The company is built on an overarching premise: "We are ladies and gentlemen serving ladies and gentlemen." This guiding principle spawns a short list of values, carried by each employee; every day a specific value is selected to receive special attention. Regular "line-ups," including cross-sections of employees, are convened weekly to tell stories and review their values.

New employees participate in an intensive two-day orientation where company leaders, hotel managers, representatives from a variety of employee ranks, and others review the Ritz-Carlton history, and present the credo, motto, and core values and tell stories to illustrate how these values play out each day in the company's properties. The two days are intense, yet fun. After twenty-one days on the job, new hires are reconvened in another intense session to review the values in the light of recent on-the-job experiences. In between the session, mentors are encouraged to help newcomers adjust. But mentoring is informal and based, in large part, on newcomers attuned to observe the behavior of others and old-timers sensitized to how what they do sends important signals about how the company's values play out every day.

A new person at one of the Ritz-Carlton Hotels commented on her recent orientation experience:

At our two-day orientation the hotel's general managers were all there. They treated us like VIPs, like ladies and gentlemen. What they were talking about was real. During the session, I watched a general manager pick up a napkin from the floor. Their deeds matched their words. They had us role-playing different situations, acting out the Service Values. I have the values of Ritz-Carlton in my heart. They are not just words; they are a philosophy to live by.

We were never assigned mentors. They are everywhere. Manny (a manager), wow! He's one of my mentors. I watch what he does. He models how to deal with guests and situations with integrity and sincerity.

An older employee recalled the highlight of her 2008 orientation experience:

It was fun, but everything we did reinforced the values. Before a break on the second day, we were asked to identify our favorite food. When we returned a large quantity of what people desired was at their place: French fries, ice cream, and hot dogs—whatever. My favorite was chocolate, and in front of my place were two pounds of Belgian dark chocolate. We all exclaimed "WOW!" Then our trainers told us to remember that gesture. Our main job, whatever our role, was to WOW our guests. That stuck with me, and I think about it every day.

As a result of this intense acculturation, the quality of guest service at Ritz-Carlton is consistently superb across employee ranks—front desk greeters, housekeepers, custodians, or dining room servers. The turnover of new employees is far lower for Ritz-Carton than other companies in the same industry.

MENTORING IN CULTURAL CONTEXT

The problem of teacher turnover in our nation's schools is as critical as it is for any set of organizations—businesses, hospitals, or other nonprofits. Mentoring has now been singled out as a way to stop the exit of new teachers from the profession. And indeed, throughout history, mentoring has loomed as one important way that a novice can master new skills and learn the ropes in an unfamiliar organization. But mentoring is only one part of the process through which newcomers are brought into the ways and practices of an existing human group. The more robust the culture, the more intense the acculturation ritual.

In many of today's schools, the cultural fabric that gives meaning and buoyancy to what goes on has been weakened by decades of state and federal reform initiatives, most aimed at making schools more rational, technical, and accountable. These constant pressures have created in some schools a cultural vacuum eroding teachers' faith and belief in what they do. In these instances, continued waves of reform have contributed to school cultures that have gone sour.

Weak cultures rob teaching of meaning; negative cultures provide meaning that is hard to justify. Less attention has been paid at the local level to fostering the kind of leadership that refocuses attention on reshaping and revitalizing the culture of schools and encouraging positive values, heroes, rituals, ceremonies, and stories. These are the crucial elements in many schools that sustain meaning, hope, and belief. From this deep existential well come the constructive acculturation practices that bring new teachers into the fold. It is the same mentality that encourages the initiation of natural mentoring relationships, built on the same premises surmised long ago. When a newcomer becomes an integral player in a new cultural milieu, they are far less likely to leave than if they have not been acculturated in a meaningful way.

For the most part, state-sponsored, formal approaches to mentoring as a way to reduce teacher turnover suffer in two respects: they separate mentoring from the process of acculturation, and they drape the essence of mentoring with rational and bureaucratic baggage.

NOTE

1. The CTC (2014) report is an agenda item that presents findings from the state-wide survey and recommendations to strengthen induction for new teachers (p. 1).

REFERENCES

Bird, T., & Little, J. W. (1986). How schools organize the teaching occupation. *Elementary School Journal 86*, 493–512.

Bolman, L. G., & Deal, T. E. (1994). *Becoming a teacher leader: From isolation to collaboration.* Thousand Oaks, CA: Sage.

California Commission on Teacher Credentialing (CTC). (August, 2014). 4F Action. *Professional services committee update on induction: State survey information and options to strengthen and stabilize induction in 2014–15 and beyond.* Sacramento, CA: Author. http://www.ctc.ca.gov/commission/agendas/2014-08/2014-08-4F.pdf.

Colley, H. (2000, September). Exploring myths of mentor: A rough guide to the history of mentoring from a Marxist feminine perspective. Paper presented at the British Educational Research Association Annual Conference, Cardiff University.

Deal, T. E., & Redman, D. (2013). Rejuvenating teacher teams: Back to basics. In *Moving from teacher isolation to collaboration: Enhancing professionalism and school quality.* Edited by S. Conley & B. S. Cooper, 35–48. Lanham, MD: Rowman & Littlefield.

Feiman-Nemser, S., & Carver, C. L. (2012). Creating conditions for serious mentoring: Implications for induction policy. *National Society for the Study of Education 111* (2), 342–64.

Hargreaves, A., & Dawe, R. (1990). Paths of professional development: Contrived collegiality, collaborative culture, and the case of peer coaching. *Teaching and Teacher Education 6* (3), 227–41.

Homer. (1945). *The Odyssey.* Penguin Books.

Howe, E. R. (2006). Exemplary teacher induction: An international review. *Educational Philosophy and Theory 38* (3), 287–97.

Huling-Austin, L. (1990). Mentoring is squishy business. *Mentoring: Developing successful new teachers,* 39–50.

Ingersoll, R. M., & Strong, M. (2011). The impact of induction and mentoring programs for beginning teachers: A critical review of the research. *Review of Educational Research 81,* 201–23.

Kahle-Piasecki, L. (2011). Making a mentoring relationship work: What is required for organizational success. *Journal of Applied Business and Economics 12* (1), 46–56.

Koppich, J. E., Humphrey, D. C., Bland, J. A., Heenan, B., McCaffery, T., Ramage, K., & Stokes, L. (2013). *California's beginning teachers: The bumpy path to a profession.* Menlo Park, CA: SRI International.

Mitchell, D. E., Scott, L. D., Hendrick, I. G., & Boyns, D. E. (1998). *The California beginning teacher support and assessment program.* 1998 Statewide Evaluation Study.

Nias, J., Southworth, G., & Yeomans, R. (1989). *Staff relationships in the primary school.* London: Cassells.

Norman, P. J., & Feiman-Nemser, S. (2005). Mind activity in teaching and mentoring. *Teaching and Teacher Education 21,* 679–97.

Pine, C. K. (2006). *Developing beginning teachers' professional capabilities in the workplace: An investigation of one California County's induction program using the success case method.* Doctoral dissertation, University of California, Santa Barbara.

Rhodes, C., & Beneicke, S. (2002). Coaching, mentoring and peer-networking: Challenges for the management of teacher professional development in schools. *Journal of In-Service Education 28* (2), 297–310.

Sun, C. (March, 2012). Teacher induction: Improving state systems for supporting new teachers. *NASBE Discussion Guide*, 1–19.

Tellez, K. (1992). Mentors by choice, not design: Help-seeking by beginning teachers. *Journal of Teacher Education 43* (3), 214–21.

Villar, A., & Strong, M. (2007). Is mentoring worth the money? A benefit-cost analysis and five-year rate of return of a comprehensive mentoring program for beginning teachers. *ERS Spectrum 25* (3), 1–17.

Waller, W. W. (1932). *The sociology of teaching*. New York: Wiley.

Chapter 6

Teacher Mentoring
Practices and Models

What Can We Learn from Research and Effective Practices?

Chun Zhang

INTRODUCTION

Having highly qualified teachers is one of the most important variables in contributing to positive student outcomes, to closing achievement gaps, and to preventing school failure (Phillips, 2010). However, new teachers need support and mentoring in the beginning years of their teaching careers for them to become highly qualified educators (Barrera, Braley, & Slate, 2010). Beginning teachers who were provided with well-structured mentoring had higher levels of student engagement than those who were not (Stanulis & Floden, 2009). Studies also indicate that rigorous, well-planned, and well-structured mentoring programs hold great potential for improving beginning teachers' practices and for affecting students' academic outcomes positively (Hobson et al., 2009; Mathur, Gehrke, & Kim, 2012; Smith & Ingersoll, 2004).

As schools and teacher education programs face the challenges of preparing and keeping highly qualified teachers—especially for low-performing urban schools—good or effective mentor characteristics and mentoring practices and models that have promise and evidence of success need to be examined and disseminated. This chapter will examine the literature and research in the areas of effective teaching, mentor characteristics, and teacher mentoring practices and models. Important indicators and characteristics of mentors and mentoring programs will be highlighted. Practical applications of how schools can conceptualize, plan, and implement successful mentoring programs will be discussed.

CHARACTERISTICS OF EFFECTIVE TEACHING

Effective teachers of high-achieving students tend to have the following five characteristics: (1) high expectations, (2) a focus on academic instruction that engages, motivates, and challenges students, (3) have smooth transitions during activities, (4) address the needs of students, and (5) connect curriculum with students' interests and experiences. These teachers are clear and enthusiastic in the delivery of instruction, and they use time effectively (Brophy & Good, 1986).

In addition, they also manage their classrooms effectively through developing routines and procedures and helping students learn self-regulation and independent thinking and problem-solving skills. They create a comfortable, intellectually stimulating, and collaborative learning environment where authentic, interesting, and challenging activities are provided. They also monitor students' learning and progress, and scaffold student learning to a deep understanding of curriculum across domains and content areas (Bogner, Raphael, & Pressley, 2002; Dolezal, Welsh, Pressley, & Vincent, 2003; Roehrig, Bohn, Turner, & Pressley, 2008).

These teaching behaviors and skills are found to be conducive to students' learning and to promoting positive student outcomes. In general, teachers' attitudes, beliefs, and knowledge affect teachers' behaviors and skills to work with their students, having an impact on students' engagement and learning. Specifically, teachers' instructional skills and practices are found to have direct effects on students' achievement, whereas other teacher characteristics such as teacher beliefs and knowledge may have an indirect impact on student learning and achievement (Roehrig et al., 2008; Muijs & Reynolds, 2002).

Today's new teachers face many challenges and need to become effective in the first few years of their teaching careers in learning the skills of planning and implementing curriculum and instruction, conducting different types of assessments, engaging and motivating students, guiding students' behaviors, and managing the classroom environments and monitoring students' progress (Roehrig, Pressley, & Talotta, 2002). With an increasing emphasis on accountability and linking teacher performance with student outcomes, today's teachers face an overwhelming amount of stress, pressure, and many challenges during the first years of teaching in learning about and performing the multifaceted tasks of teaching (Roehrig et al., 2002). With the pressure to perform and have their students excel while managing the high demands of daily classroom teaching, beginning teachers may feel stressed out or burned out if left out without support and mentoring (Roehrig et al., 2008).

Having well-prepared and highly qualified teachers in every classroom is the best and most consistent predictor of positive student performance and achievement (Barrera, Braley, & Slate, 2010; Phillips, 2010). Many studies concluded that teachers are one of the most important factors that explain the variation in students' achievement in the form of test scores (Goldhaber & Brewer, 1997; Phillips, 2010). Teachers at the beginning of their teaching careers need support and mentoring for them to become accustomed to the school culture and to have a confident handle on the instruction and class-room management to be able to support students individually and as a group.

Teacher mentoring is crucial for nurturing and supporting beginning teachers to stay in the profession and for helping them acquire skills to become highly qualified and effective educators and teacher leaders. Mentoring programs, when thoughtfully conceptualized, well structured, and effectively delivered, can greatly improve the skills of beginning teachers (Barrera, Braley, & Slate, 2010).

CHARACTERISTICS OF GOOD MENTORS AND MENTORING

Barrera et al. (2010) explained that mentoring occurs when a colleague who has more experience and skill provides information, advice, and emotional support to a mentee over an extended period of time. This mentoring relationship involves a substantial commitment from both parties (Mullen, 2005). For the mentoring to be effective, mentors need to provide ample time, develop trust, be willing to listen and learn—and have an ability to encourage and guide mentees.

Teacher leaders also need to be open minded and recognize the limitations of their mentees (e.g., a lack of experience in working with children and inadequate knowledge about the operations of schools) without being judgmental, controlling, or criticizing (Madison, Watson, & Knight, 1994). Brown, Katz, Hargrove, and Hill (2003) emphasized the characteristics of mentors and stated that effective mentors are sincere, approachable, demonstrate active listening skills, and maintain integrity. They are willing to spend time with their mentees while being enthusiastic and positive about their mentor roles. Other characteristics of mentors include being flexible, tactful, trustworthy, and confidential. To have these qualities and skills, mentors need preparation and training in their mentoring roles and responsibilities (Barrera et al., 2010; Holloway, 2001).

Good mentors play a very important role in helping develop their mentees' professional competence through providing different levels of personal, professional, and organizational support (McIntyre & Hagger, 1996). In particular, good mentors help mentees share domains of expertise, develop interpersonal relationships, and transfer new knowledge development (Hennissen, Crasborn, Brouwer, Korthagen, & Bergen, 2011). Several researchers examined attributes or characteristics of good mentors. Good mentors are considered as a source of new knowledge for mentees. They possess a good amount of subject matter knowledge. They can translate their theoretical knowledge and enhance mentees' learning and teaching (Little, 1990; Roberts, 2000).

Moreover, good mentors have rich pedagogical content knowledge. They can explain and model problem solving in clear and deep ways to help mentees understand patterns, and at the same time, infuse personal sources of information to help mentees understand and solve dilemmas they encounter (Brown, 2001; Berliner, 2001). Thus, a combination of subject matter knowledge and pedagogical skills enables mentors to help mentees connect among theory, practice, and research within the context of the mentees' needs and situations (Feiman-Nemser & Folden, 1986; Orland-Barak & Hasin, 2010; Vonk, 1993).

Rowley (1999) further identified good or effective mentor characteristics. For example, he explained that good mentors act as role models for lifelong learning; they are open and transparent, and they themselves strive for lifelong learning from other colleagues and for professional growth; and they engage in learning about best practices and new initiatives such as new curricula. Other researchers (Cochran-Smith & Paris, 1992; Feiman-Nemser, 2001; Shandley, 1989) found that good mentors engage in processes that create interpersonal relationships based on trust, collaboration, and support—aimed at social and professional change in the mentoring process (Belenky, Clinchy, Goldberger, & Tarule, 1986; Cochran-Smith & Paris, 1992; Elliott & Calderhead, 1993; McIntyre & Hagger, 1996). They also create opportunities that foster professional development and improve their teaching capacities for themselves and for mentees (Tomlinson, 2001; Wang, 2001).

CHARACTERISTICS OF EFFECTIVE MENTORING

Mentoring can consist of modeling and instructing, co-planning and brainstorming, supervising, evaluating mentoring, and learning from each other (Zanting, Verloop, Vermunt, & Van Driel, 1998). Good mentoring practices for new and experienced teachers at both the preservice and in-service levels should be a developmental and nurturing process, whereby mentors guide and lead mentees in developing their professional competence and identity (McIntyre & Hagger, 1996).

Mentoring has been examined by different researchers and included different components. Huffman and Leak (1986), for example, examined mentoring at three areas of assistance for beginning teachers: providing encouragement, support, and collegiality; giving specific suggestions for improving teaching; and giving feedback and evaluation. Lindgren (2005) studied two areas of assistance: personal/emotional and professional. Professional assistance was related to asking questions and giving feedback. Ballantyne, Hansford, and Packer (1995) categorized mentoring into four areas of assistance: (1) offering empathy and reassurance, (2) providing task-related assistance such as giving advice and useful information, (3) giving problem-related assistance and advice through discussion and exploration of problems, and (4) facilitating critical reflection and feedback on practice.

Although different researchers examined mentoring from different areas of assistance, all of these types of assistance are perceived important by mentees: (1) emotional support is viewed critical because mentees want to have access to mentors who they can trust and provide positive support; (2) task-related support can enhance beginning teachers' teaching skills, which include giving information, practical advice, and feedback; and (3) asking questions and discussing topics/areas regarding different aspects of teaching that mentees need (Hennissen et al., 2011).

EFFECTIVE MENTORING PRACTICES AND PROGRAMS

Five stages are relevant to the process of developing a teacher mentoring program in schools today (Sindelar, 1992). The stages involve establishing a rationale, selecting mentors and mentees, training mentors, monitoring the mentoring process, and evaluating and revising the mentoring program (Barrera et al., 2010; Norman & Ganser, 2004).

Norman and Ganser (2004) observed that mentoring practices and programs have changed significantly in the last decade. They mentioned that in the past, mentoring programs were considered as an optional type of assistance for new teachers, usually in the form of providing information about policies and procedures of local schools. In recent years, mentoring programs were required of new teachers. In some states, the State Department of Education requires new teachers to have mentoring in the first year of teaching. Wang and Odell (2002) indicated that these mentoring roles and activities were linked to external standards, as more and more states are in the process of implementing standards-based curriculum such as Common Core standards. Thus, natural mentoring or optional mentoring in the past has been replaced by mentoring that has been heavily influenced by external standards and expectations about what teachers should know and do in order to prepare students to meet the external standards.

These changes imply that *mentoring* will need to be structured and organized to prepare and support new teachers and/or experienced teachers who are not familiar with these requirements or standards. Also, *mentoring programs* to help new teachers develop effective teaching practices should be in place as well (Mathur, Gehrke, & Kim, 2012). Structurally, mentoring programs need to consider logistical planning that include the following:

(1) clarifying the type of mentoring structures, (2) allowing time for observations and frequency of contact, and (3) matching process between mentors and mentees (Kardos & Moore Johnson, 2007).

Barrera et al. (2010) found that mentoring programs need to have clearly defined goals, roles, and responsibilities of mentors and mentees and evaluation by relevant stakeholders to determine the effectiveness of the mentoring programs. Ongoing evaluations of mentoring with the goal to support mentors and mentees should be in place to improve teacher effectiveness, resulting in teachers' greater retention and thus more highly qualified teachers for all students.

In the process of developing an effective mentoring program, mentors are also developed into teacher leaders who can help new teachers translate theoretical knowledge into practical skills. Thus, a mentoring program should be conceptualized and developed not just to help new teachers to improve their teaching and classroom management skills but also to promote a teacher leader system that can help all teachers and other professionals change schools' culture and build a sustainable support system for improving teacher effectiveness and student outcomes (Orland-Barak & Hasin, 2010).

TEACHER LEADERSHIP DEVELOPMENT

Good mentors act as role models for their peers and new teachers. They are open to learning from colleagues and other sources; they are engaged in professional development in the form of reading about new practices and research, curriculum, and new initiatives in education to promote and reinforce effective practices or to explore new ways of improving teaching and learning (i.e., integrating technology to expand teaching and learning) (Rowley, 1999). Effective mentors, teachers, and teacher leaders have many qualities in common. Researchers identified many common characteristics between good mentoring, good teaching, and quality teacher leadership (Hennissen et al., 2011; Orland-Barak & Hasin, 2010). Vonk (1993) found that effective teachers and mentors can effectively make connections between theory and practical knowledge. They have pedagogical and content knowledge, and they can explain complicated concepts and problems clearly and effectively (Shulman, 1986).

When serving as mentors, they could explain, model, and link what they observed in their mentee's teaching to theoretical, pedagogical, and didactic applications. Mentors and effective teachers also possessed the ability to develop and promote positive classroom environments for their students

(Cochran-Smith & Paris, 1992; McIntyre & Hagger, 1996; Roberts, 2000; Rowley, 1999).

Effective teachers and mentors also demonstrate great organizational skills. They can manage time, setting, planning, and teaching effectively (Haberman, 1995). Miles, Saxl, and Lieberman (1988) found that many mentors possess qualities and skills that distinguish them as leaders who think and act as leaders in schools. They are knowledgeable, experienced, organized, and are risk takers; and they have strong interpersonal and communication skills. Many mentors acted as leaders and had the ability to motivate and empower their mentees, promoting autonomous practices, independent decision making and problem solving, and reflective practices among their peers and mentees (Bass, 1985; Burns, 1978; Popper, 2001; Popper, Mayseless, & Castelnovo, 2000).

EXAMPLES OF MENTORING MODELS IN EDUCATION AND BUSINESS

Most mentoring programs are structured and developed to help new teachers. Different mentoring programs are developed for different purposes. Three examples will be discussed below. The first type of mentoring program was designed to implement a new literacy curriculum aimed at improving the literacy instructional practices of teachers and early reading skills of young children. Mentors modeled and implemented early literacy activities in collaboration with classroom teachers and co-planned curriculum in the process of implementing a research-based literacy project with the hope of improving the oral language and early literacy skills of young children (Zoll & Rosenquest, 2011). Such a mentoring program is designed to address a specific need in a curriculum and in the skill sets of teachers and students.

The second type of mentoring program introduced by Portner included organizational structures/components for defining the multiple functions of mentoring (Portner, 2008). He described four essential components/functions of mentoring. They are relating, assessing, coaching, and guiding. As mentors develop relationships with mentees, they need to emphasize mutual trust, respect, and professionalism. In the assessing process, mentors and mentees need to be engaged in gathering and diagnosing data regarding mentees' needs and professional development within the context of the district's and school's expectations for student success.

Based on the needs assessment, mentors will model and share examples and strategies to help mentees learn, reflect, and enhance their grasp of content and pedagogical skills. As mentors and mentees are mutually and actively engaged in the discussions about issues and strategies, mentors will guide mentees to develop critical-thinking and problem-solving skills to help mentees develop professional competence and identity and empower mentees to make critical decisions in the multidimensions of their teaching in the areas of instruction, assessment, classroom management, and data-based decisions in daily classroom teaching to support positive student outcomes.

The third type of mentoring model in business described by Johnson (1997) emphasized the use of mentoring for achieving personal, team, and organizational excellence. He proposed these three levels of excellence, and each level influences the other. The strategic mentoring model targets learning, leading, and relating at the individual, group/team, and organization levels. In this model, the individual needs to facilitate continuous individual learning, individual leadership development, and individual relationship-building skills. At the group/team level, the group/team needs to facilitate continuous learning on building team excellence, team leadership development, and developing team-relationship-building skills.

At the organization level, the organization needs to facilitate the development of a learning organization, nurtures the leadership development at all levels, and builds a culture that emphasizes positive working relationships. The goal of this strategic mentoring model is to support every member to achieve excellence at the individual, group/team, and the organization levels, resulting in positive relationships and outcomes for all members of a learning organization that grows and improves itself. This type of systematic mentoring model is an ideal model that should be promoted in all schools and organizations.

IMPLICATIONS FOR TEACHER MENTORING AND TEACHER LEADERSHIP DEVELOPMENT

As more external standards and demands are required of teachers and schools, schools need to be proactive in creating a safe, trusting, and supportive environment for teachers and administrators to be engaged in designing mentoring programs collaboratively. These demands mean the goals of the mentoring programs need to be consistent with teacher development and student outcomes. Mentors and mentees should be matched thoughtfully so that mentees can form a trusting relationship with their mentors as they learn about the school culture, navigate the systems, learn and improve their teaching and classroom management skills, and develop their professional identify and styles.

In today's educational contexts, teachers, administrators, and students feel more demands and pressure. Within the context of standard-based curriculum and outcome-based accountability, good teaching cannot be replaced by rigid test preparation and sheer compliance with external standards. Good teaching and learning needs to be the soul of teaching that should be "infused with pleasure, passion, creativity, challenge, and joy" (Hargreaves, 1997, p. 12), for both teachers and students.

Thus, mentoring needs to involve helping mentees learn and use the standards and tactfully integrate them within the skillful teaching practices and processes. More importantly, mentoring needs to model passion and excitement in the teaching process and provide emotional support and encouragement to nurture new teachers into the teaching profession and to prepare them to be the next generation of teacher leaders for the success of students and the education enterprise as a whole (Norman & Ganser, 2004).

REFERENCES

Ballantyne, R., Hansford, B., & Packer, J. (1995). Mentoring beginning teachers: A qualitative analysis of process and outcomes. *Educational Review 47* (3), 297–306.

Barrera, A., Braley, R. T., & Slate, J. R. (2010). Beginning teacher success: An investigation into the feedback from mentors of formal mentoring programs. *Mentoring & Tutoring: Partnership in Learning 18* (1), 61–74.

Bass, B. M. (1985). *Leadership and performance beyond expectation.* New York: Free Press.

Belenky, M. F., Clinchy, B. M., Goldberger, N. R., & Tarule, J. M. (1986). *Women's ways of knowing: The development of self, voice, and mind.* New York: Basic Books.

Berliner, C. D. (2001). Learning about and learning from expert teachers. *International Journal of Educational Research 35*, 463–82.

Bogner, K., Raphael, L. M., & Pressley, M. (2002). How grade 1 teachers motivate literate activity by their students. *Scientific Studies of Reading 6*, 135–65.

Brophy, J., & Good, T. (1986). Teacher behavior and student achievement. In *Handbook of research on teaching.* Edited by M. Wittrock, 340–70. New York: Macmillan.

Brown, K. (2001). Mentoring and the retention of newly qualified language teachers. *Cambridge Journal of Education 31*, 69–88.

Brown, T., Hargrove, S., Hill, R., & Katz, L. (2003). Promoting quality teachers through a supportive mentoring environment for pre-service and first-year teachers. Paper presented at the annual Meeting of the Association for Teacher Educators (Santa Fe, NM, August 9–13, 2003). ED 480 857.

Burns, J. M. (1978). *Leadership.* New York: Harper & Row.

Cochran-Smith, M., & Paris, C. L. (1992). *Mentor and mentoring: Did Homer have it right?* Paper presented at the annual meeting of the American Educational Research Association. San Francisco.

Dolezal, S. E., Welsh, L. M., Pressley, M., & Vincent, M. M. (2003). How nine third-grade teachers motivate student academic engagement. *Elementary School Journal 103*, 239–67.

Elliott, B., & Calderhead, J. (1993). *Mentoring for teacher development: Possibilities and caveats.* In *Mentoring: Perspectives on school-based teacher education.* Edited by D. McIntyre, H. Hagger, & M. Wilkin, 166–89. London: Kogan Page.

Feiman-Nemser, S. (2001). From preparation to practice: Designing a continuum to strengthen and sustain teaching. *Teachers College Record 103* (6), 1013–55.

Feiman-Nemser, S., & Folden, R. (1986). The cultures of teaching. In *Handbook of research on teaching*, 3rd edition. Edited by M. Wittrock, 505–26. New York: Macmillan.

Goldhaber, D. D., & Brewer, D. J. (1997). Why don't schools and teachers seem to matter? Assessing the impact of unobservables on education productivity. *Journal of Human Resources 32* (3), 505–23.

Haberman, M. (1995). *Star teachers of children in poverty.* West Lafayette, IN: Kappa Delta Pi.

Hargreaves, A. (1997). *Rethinking educational change: Going deeper and wider in the quest for success.* In *Rethinking educational change with heart and mind.* Edited by A. Hargreaves, 1–26. Reston, VA: Association for Supervision and Curriculum Development.

Hennissen, P., Crasborn, F., Brouwer, N., Korthagen, F., & Bergen, T. (2011). Clarifying pre-service teacher perceptions of mentor teachers' developing use of mentoring skills. *Teaching and Teacher Education 27*, 1049–58.

Hiiffam, G., & Leak, S. (1986). Beginning teachers' perceptions of mentors. *Journal of Teacher Education 37*, 22–25.

Hobson, A., Ashby, P., Malderez, A., & Tomlinson, P. (2009). Mentoring beginning teachers: What we know and what we don't. *Teaching and Teacher Education 25*, 207–16.

Holloway, J. H. (2001). The benefits of mentoring. *Educational Leadership 58* (8), 85–86.

Huffman, G. & Leak, S. (1986). Beginning teachers' perceptions of mentors. *Journal of Teacher Education 37*, 22–25.

Johnson, H. E. (1997). *Mentoring for exceptional excellence.* Glendale, CA: Griffin Publishing.

Kardos, S., & Moore Johnson, S. (2007). On their own and presumed expert: New teachers' experience with their colleagues. *The Teachers College Record 109* (9), 2083–2106.

Lindgren, U. (2005). Experiences of beginning teachers in a school-based mentoring program in Sweden. *Educational Studies 31*, 251–63.

Little, J. W. (1990). The mentor phenomenon and the social organization of teaching. In *Review of research in education.* Edited by C. B. Cazden, *16*, 297–350. Washington, DC: AREA.

Madison, J., Watson, K., & Knight, B. (1994). Mentors and preceptors in the nursing profession. *Contemporary Nurse 3* (3), 121–26.

Mathur, S. R., Gehrke, R., & Kim, S. H. (2012). Impact of a teacher mentorship program on mentors' and mentees' perceptions of classroom practices and the mentoring experience. *Assessment for Effective Intervention 38* (3), 154–62.

McIntyre, D. & Hagger, H. (Eds.) (1996) *Mentors in schools: Developing the profession of teaching.* London: David Fulton Publishing.

McIntyre, D., Hagger, H., & Wilkin, M. (2005). *Mentoring: Perspectives on school-based teacher education.* London: Routledge Falmer.

Miles, M., Saxl, E., & Lieberman, A. (1988). What skills do educational "change agents" need? An empirical view. *Curriculum Inquiry 18* (2), 157–93.

Muijs, D., & Reynolds, D. (2002). Teachers' beliefs and behaviors: What really matters? *Journal of Classroom Interaction 37* (2), 3–15.

Mullen, C. A. (2005). *The mentorship primer.* New York: Peter Lang.

Norman, D. M., & Ganser, T. (2004). A humanistic approach to new teacher mentoring: A counseling perspective. *Journal of Humanistic Counseling, Education and Development 43*, 129–40.

Orland-Barak, L., & Hasin, R. (2010). Exemplary mentors' perspectives towards mentoring across mentoring contexts: Lessons from collective case studies. *Teaching and Teacher Education 26*, 427–37.

Phillips (K. J. R.) (2010). What does "highly qualified" mean for student achievement? Evaluating the relationships between teacher quality indicators and at-risk students' mathematics and reading achievement gains in first grade. *Elementary School Journal 110* (4), 464–93.

Popper, M. (2001). *Hypnotic leadership: Leaders, followers and the loss of self.* Westport, CT: Praeger.

Popper, M., Mayseless, O., & Castelnovo, O. (2000). Transformational leadership and attachment. *Leadership Quarterly 11*, 267–89.

Portner, H. (2008). *Mentoring new teachers*, 3rd Edition. Thousand Oaks, CA: Corwin Press.

Roberts, A. (2000). Mentoring revisited: A phenomenological reading of the literature. *Mentoring & Tutoring 8* (2), 145–70.

Roehrig, A. D., Bohn, C. M., Turner, J. Z., & Pressley, M. (2008). Mentoring beginning primary teachers for exemplary teaching practices. *Teaching and Teacher Education 24*, 684–702.

Roehrig, A. D., Pressley, M., & Talotta, D. A. (2002). *Stories of beginning teachers: First-year challenges and beyond.* Notre Dame, IN: University of Notre Dame Press.

Rowley, J. B. (1999). The good mentor. *Educational Leadership 56* (8), 20–22.

Shandley, T. C. (1989). The use of mentors for leadership development. *NASPA 27*, 59–66.

Shulman, L. S. (1986). Those who understand: Knowledge growth in teaching. *Educational Researcher 15* (2), 4–14.

Sindelar, N. (1992). Development of a teacher mentorship program: High professionalism and low cost. *ERS Spectrum 10* (2), 13–17.

Smith, T., & Ingersoll, R. (2004). What are the effects of induction and mentoring on beginning teacher turnover? *American Educational Research Journal 41*, 681–84.

Stanulis, R., & Floden, R. (2009). Intensive mentoring as a way to help beginning teachers develop balanced instruction. *Journal of Teacher Education 60*, 112–22.

Tomlinson, P. (2001). *Understanding mentoring: Reflective strategies for school-based teacher education.* Buckingham, UK: Open University Press.

Vonk, J. H. C. (1993). Mentoring beginning teachers: Mentor knowledge and skills. *Mentoring and Tutoring 1* (1), 31–41.

Wang, J. (2001). Contexts of mentoring and opportunities for learning to teach: A comparative study of mentoring practice. *Teaching and Teacher Education 17*, 51–73.

Wang, J., & Odell, S. J. (2002). Mentored learning to teach according to standards-based reform: A critical review. *Review of Educational Research 72*, 481–46.

Zanting, A., Verloop, J. D., Vermunt, J. D., & Van Driel, J. H. (1998). Explicating practical knowledge: An extension of mentor teachers' roles. *European Journal of Teacher Education 21* (1), 11–28.

Zoll, S. M., & Rosenquest, B. (2011). Sustainable practices in mentoring: Tools to support child outcomes and a mentoring protocol in early language and literacy. *NHSA Dialog 14* (4), 213–28.

Chapter 7

Mentoring College Students with Disabilities

Processes and Programs

Carol Strax and Marshall Strax

Meghan arrived on campus with excitement and great expectations for her future. She looked up at the ivy-draped buildings framed by the blue August sky and knew she had arrived at the place of her dreams. The admissions personnel had assured her that State U would provide her with an environment of Universal Design for Learning (UDL), including all the accommodations for learning and access she had received in high school.

INTRODUCTION

The idea of mentoring has been around since the time of Homer, with various types and models of mentoring including individual, group, peer, professional, and electronic. This chapter discusses the types and models of mentoring endemic to postsecondary education, particularly for college students with disabilities—and the reasons for its importance.

"Mentoring is a dynamic, reciprocal, long-term formal or informal relationship that focuses on personal and/or professional development. A mentor is a sounding board and guide. Mentors provide perspectives and resources and ask thought-provoking questions" (Foster Heckman, Brown, & Roberts, 2007, p. 2). The quality of a mentoring program can make or break postsecondary *students with disabilities* (SWD).

"Understanding what characteristics lead to effective mentors and mentoring programs may enhance the enrollment, retention, and matriculation rates of students with disabilities attending postsecondary institutions" (Brown, Takahashi, & Roberts, 2010, p. 110). Lightner, Kipps-Vaughn, Schulte, and Trice (2012) suggest that receiving mentoring through a Disability Support

Services (DSS) program made a significant difference in credits earned and grade point average by the middle of the sophomore year. SWD who received mentoring were more likely to graduate college (Troiano, Liefeld, & Trachtenberg, 2010) than those who did not receive mentoring through DSS.

Transitions from high school to postsecondary institutions of learning can pose a number of problems for young adults with disabilities. Unlike high schools where SWD fall under the umbrella of the Individuals with Disabilities Education Act (IDEA) (2006), postsecondary schools are governed by three other statues—Section 504 of the Rehabilitation Act (2006), the Americans with Disabilities Act (ADA) (2006), and the Higher Education Opportunity Act (HEOA) (2008)—which mandate that postsecondary institutions provide a nondiscriminatory educational environment for all SWD who are otherwise qualified to participate in all programs offered, including full access to all facilities, technology, and social and extracurricular activities along with athletic programs and events.

Under these statutes, SWD are held responsible to self-disclose their disabilities and find appropriate services; it is not the postsecondary school's responsibility to assess, identify, and classify SWD and provide remedial education, related services, and accommodations. SWD are left to fend for themselves (Brown, Takahashi, & Roberts, 2010), have a lack of knowledge about how their disability is diagnosed, and how services for SWD differ between high school and college (Lightner, Kipps-Vaughn, Schulte, & Trice, 2012).

One in four college students with disabilities recount not receiving the appropriate accommodations needed for academic success (National Center for Education Statistics [NCES], 2003). Forty-three percent of students without disabilities aged twenty-five to sixty-four graduated from college, compared with 32.5 percent of those with mild and moderate disabilities and only 21.9 percent of those with severe disabilities (National Council on Disability [NCD], 2005).

Students' success and retention have a high correlation to appropriate accommodations and mentoring supports in postsecondary schools (Mull, Sitlington, & Alper, 2001). While colleges and universities are required to provide appropriate accommodations and mentoring supports, they do not have to give services for those that impose an unfair burden on the institution or alter a program of study. Various institutions interpret this ruling differently. The types of programs available to SWD can be vastly different.

According to Lightner, Kipps-Vaughn, Schulte, and Trice (2012), students receiving more transition services in high school were more proactive in using DSS in college. Students with less knowledge of the benefits of mentoring sought services usually only after problems surfaced—and did not understand the reasons for maintaining disability status in college. The primary reason for seeking DSS was academic failure or near failure, preventing participation in other activities.

Students transitioning to college need to be provided with information about services offered by DSS and be encouraged by high school transition counselors and parents to seek out those needed services. SWD are overwhelmed by the amount of information both electronic and interpersonal in orientation programs that they received when arriving at campus as freshman, and they often missed the most important information for them—the availability of mentoring opportunities through DSS.

A college degree is necessary for people with disabilities to be competitive in the current labor market (Gil, 2007). Postsecondary institutions can best support SWD by providing mentoring programs to ensure full participation in all DSS on campus and assistance in navigating the campus environment (Brown, Takahashi, & Roberts, 2010; Pingry O'Neill, Markward, & French, 2012). Colleges should provide institution-specific information about all DSS—which are all about mentoring—made available on campus and tell folks how to access them to ensure that all SWD receive the information, not just those who come forward.

According to the National Center for Special Education Research (2011), 60 percent of young adults with disabilities continue to postsecondary education, and only approximately 28 percent disclose their disability. The National Center for Education Statistics (NCES) (2006) reports that there are more than 1.4 million students attending college with documented disabilities in postsecondary education. The importance of developing ideal mentoring programs are the following: (1) to support the academic and psychosocial needs of these students, (2) to avoid voluntary and involuntary withdrawal, and thus (3) to increase retention and graduation rates of institutions (Thompson-Ebanks, 2014). Mentorship programs may likely increase success in college (Stumbo, Lindahl-Lewis, & Blegen, 2008).

MENTOR AND MENTEE RELATIONSHIPS

Mentoring is a complex, personal, and interpersonal process. Rogers (1961; 1970) and Noddings (1984) provide an excellent theoretical foundation on which to build mentor and mentee or protégé relationships. Rogers believed in a person-centered approach to building a powerful working relationship between two people in a therapeutic relationship. With unconditional positive regard—that is, each party meeting the other with no preconceived beliefs about the others' personhood—an authentic, honest, and open relationship can be established. In a two-way Rogerian relationship, vulnerabilities and strengths are laid bare, mutual trust is created, and a *reciprocal I-Thou* bond is created where participants can freely move in and out of the mentor-mentee role. Thus, the relationship is fluid, constantly changing, and evolving as the mentor and mentee work through crises, conflicts, and their resolutions, becoming increasingly intimate. If the socioemotional bond is not established, the relationship is often hampered by a lack of trust.

Noddings (1984) charges mentors of adults with disabilities to create caring relationships with their mentees. In a caring relationship, student potential is maximized, reciprocal relationships and mutual trusts are created, and the needs of the mentee are the end of all decision making, not a means to some others' end. Mentor and protégé learn from each other (Foster Heckman, Brown, & Roberts, 2007) in a cyclical relationship continually evolving into more meaningful and useful levels of caring. Davis (1997) believes the powerful voices of people with disabilities need to be heard. Mentors and mentees—either or both with disabilities—meeting in the *here and now* while practicing active listening can create more useful working relationships.

Upon entering postsecondary education, SWD are metaphorically asked to take a "leap into nothingness" (Fingarette, 1963, p. 101)—to enter a world where they have never been and in which they have no idea what they will encounter—and disclose who they are and navigate a new terrain to access the services needed for survival. Negative stigmas about disability still exist (Patrick & Wessel, 2013). Society's cultural perceptions are partly to blame.

A clash of cultures can exist when SWD are working with mentors without disabilities. Negotiating the borderlines between the culture of disability and other cultures becomes the first task of the relationships, as mentors and mentees resolve the cultural differences that may negatively impact their rapport. This problem may require culture brokering (Brown, Takahashi, & Roberts, 2010) to enable participants to understand and work through their differences in the beliefs, expectations, and attitudes concerning DSS. Faculty, staff, and student mentors without disabilities need to understand the unique history and life experiences of SWD as they approach the challenges of college and process the reality that the disability—part of whom their mentees are—only needs appropriate supports to succeed.

MENTORS

Ideally, mentors—professional, faculty, near-peer, and peer—are caring, person-centered individuals, with nondiscriminatory attitudes toward people. The most distinguishing factors between types of mentors are their area of expertise, level of education, and experience. Social/emotional mentoring is provided by counselors with advanced degrees, and ideally, state licensing. Life coaches, certified by an appropriate coaching association, offer coaching to improve executive functioning. Counselors with advanced degrees can supply career counseling. Faculty are excellent sources of networking opportunities, career counseling, and available advanced education opportunities in their respective areas.

Special education teachers and others trained in providing remedial education, tutoring, and academic support for SWD make excellent mentors. Faculty with expertise in *universal design for learning* (UDL)—the ideal pedagogy delivering multiple means of representation, expression, and engagement for SWD—can mentor other faculty to enable them to bring UDL into their teaching. An expert fund of subject area knowledge is needed. Professional-level academic mentors with college degrees can provide pedagogical training to employee, volunteer, and peer mentors with subject area knowledge. An expert in assistive technology will guide SWD in the use of the myriad technologies now available.

Mentors with this variety of characteristics are often currently employed and available in institutions. Current students in a variety of programs—education, special education, counseling, psychology, social work, occupational therapy, and speech and language pathology—who possess expertise and background in atypical cognitive development are excellent potential peer mentors (Davis, 2012).

Disability Support Services professionals must master the skills, attitudes, and behaviors necessary to successfully mentor SWD. Often, people are hired into positions in disability services with little knowledge about, and experience working with, SWD. Assuming competence, colleges and universities seldom provide modeling, support, or mentoring to DSS professionals. Ryan (2014) pointed out that "mentors would benefit from increased training on evidence-based interventions and supports to facilitate authentic friendships and academic success for students with Intellectual Disabilities" (p. 26). By logical extension, training and support should be offered to mentors of students with all disabilities, not just students with intellectual disabilities (ID).

Rather than pursue cavalier behaviors when hiring DSS providers, postsecondary institutions should seek to hire only those whose primary interest or career goal is to be a mentor to SWD. To recruit quality mentors, colleges and universities need to offer salaries—and possibly academic rank—commensurate with the mentor's level of education, experience, and expertise.

Mentors are responsible for maintaining confidentiality of mentee records in accordance with the professional standards of ethics of their profession. They should conscientiously pursue continuing education in their academic disciplines or professional area of licensure. Only by being an expert on the cutting edge of their fields can they provide a superior mentoring relationship to their protégés. Knowledgeable of legislation and litigation concerning postsecondary SWD, mentors must maintain legal compliance in their behaviors and all services provided.

Duties include assessing the need for appropriate services for mentees and arranging for the provision of all services. Even though role modeling self-advocacy for students, mentors still must be available to intervene with faculty and others on campus to negotiate appropriate accommodations and services for students when necessary—for example, with faculty who refuse to support these or any students.

As a one-stop person for all student needs, mentors communicate the needs of SWD with the college community as necessary and guide students in creating disability-themed clubs and support groups that may include students without disabilities on campus. In addition, mentors can organize programs and panels for presentations to the college community, including professors, counselors, administrators, and the greater community. Faculty mentors should conduct research with mentees, and shepherd them into the professional world of their discipline by accompanying them to scholarly conferences and introducing them to colleagues.

MENTEES

Ideally, mentees—students with both visible and invisible disabilities—are students who come forward upon acceptance into college or at the beginning of their first semester in college, disclose their disability, and provide documentation of diagnosis and accommodations and supports they have previously received. However, the majority of SWD either prefer not to disclose their disabilities, or due to inadequate transition planning from high school, have no knowledge of the DSS mentoring resources available to them on campus.

Many SWD eventually come forward during their first major academic and/or social crisis. Others never come forward, end up voluntarily or involuntary dropping out of college, and do not reach their academic potential. Had the students come to DSS early on, mentoring could have prevented these crises or enabled the students to work through them.

Going to college is a major life transition for all students, especially those with disabilities. Full responsibility to disclose a disability, seek evaluation and diagnosis for a previously unknown disability, arrange necessary accommodations and services, and participate in self-advocacy are new survival skills that were not needed in high school where they were provided by school personnel and parents. Mentors, even peer and faculty mentors, can help to ameliorate mentees' fears about disclosure of their disabilities and assist them in seeking out DSS. Where further assistance is available to become independent adults, mentees learn self-advocacy and about college policies concerning disability. SWD thus master how to get around campus, access campus facilities, and cope with architectural barriers and inclement weather (Patrick & Wessel, 2013).

SWD need to be active members of the academic and social systems of their college. Participation in one system, however, does not inherently imply integration into the others (Patrick & Wessel, 2013). Mentees with disabilities need advice on a variety of topics to which to belong, such as social and academic adjustment, awareness of campus resources, getting to know the faculty, and individual academic and social support. Being in companionship with other people with disabilities provides them with a support system and enhances their social transition to college.

The mentoring relationship constructively affects their transition. Those with a close relationship were more likely to listen to their mentor and use campus resources wisely. According to Thompson-Ebanks (2014),

> The participants' ability to have confidence, manage their disabilities and advocate on their own behalf, and maintain financial security was intertwined with other factors such as their perception of societal views of their disabilities, financial and institutional policies, and parental expectations. (p. 205)

Any effort to support the student should be a collective one involving administrators, faculty, staff, and peers—all potential mentors.

Mentees with disabilities withdraw from a college for a variety of reasons. Some SWD are released for academic or social reasons. Perhaps expert mentoring could have prevented dismissal. Others voluntarily withdraw for personal reasons such as disability characteristics, medical issues, feelings of inadequacy, little sense of belonging, insecure limited finances due to the impact of smaller semester courseloads on the financial aid needed for extra semesters, and the lack of involvement in campus social life (Thompson-Ebanks, 2014).

Negative environmental influences such as faculty attitudes, institutional policies, stigmas, and peer behaviors leading to reduced self-esteem, feelings of inadequacy, and student perception of systemic stigma toward people with disabilities cause some SWD to withdraw (Thompson-Ebanks, 2014). Some students, when failing courses, choose voluntarily to withdraw before they are dismissed. "The complex interconnectedness of a number of the factors is central to many of the participants' experiences emphasizing the need for a multifaceted approach to retention strategies for Students with Intellectual Disabilities" (Thompson-Ebanks, 2014, p. 195). A comprehensive mentoring program can meet mentees' needs and increase retention and student success.

Peer and near-peer mentors—especially those with disabilities—are in a unique position to answer questions that mentees may have concerning faculty, staff, courses, programs, and activities on campus that professional mentors are not at liberty to discuss or cannot answer, such as information about faculty who are resistant to accommodations. Mentors can share their experiences on campus.

Specific needs of mentees include time and stress management, assistive technology, study and test-taking skills and accommodations, note-taking assistance, organizational competence, constructive corrective feedback, appropriate executive functioning skills, and the ability to self-advocate. Academic accommodations will be needed to address deficits in listening comprehension, reading, and writing and to provide flexibility in assignment and test date deadlines.

Mentees are responsible for punctually attending all counseling and tutoring appointments, scheduled classes, timely responses to correspondence, and reporting feedback from professors and other college staff. When there is a problem—academic, medical, and psychological—they are responsible to come to DSS in a timely manner, inform their mentor of the problem, and participate in all agreed-on mentoring activities including individual, group, and whole-class mentoring.

MENTORING PROGRAMS

Mentoring programs for SWD are myriad and varied. As the ADA mandates reasonable accommodations and equal access to college life, almost all institutions provide some sort of program at no cost to students. Mentoring programs vary in depth and breadth, based on the philosophy of the college and funds available at each individual institution. Following are the descriptions of five categories of mentoring programs for SWD. Please keep in mind many variations and combinations of the five basic categories exist.

Category One: To comply with federal legislation, many institutions of higher learning offer students a floor of minimum mentoring opportunity—the most bare-bones DSS. Programs include one or more DSS personnel to evaluate student documentation of disability and to create and disseminate to necessary faculty the accommodations to learning the student is entitled to. In addition, the student can take advantage of tutoring services in some type of learning resource center open to the entire student body. Services are provided at no cost to the student.

It is now October. Meghan is failing three of her five courses. The DSS office is so short-staffed, the waiting list for appointments is over one week—she cannot get mentoring when she needs it. One hour a week of tutor-ing per course was not enough for her to succeed. State U did not have any of the assistive technology Meghan depended on. Due to inadequate mentoring, in December she will leave State U with a grade point average (GPA) of 1.2 and thousands of dollars of debt.

Category Two: In addition to bare-bones services, many institutions offer enhanced DSS at no cost to students. Additional professional and peer men-tors and technology are made available sometimes through the generosity of the college but more often through TRIO grant-funded programs—federally funded mentoring programs. These programs provide professional academic and psychosocial mentoring, far greater hours of peer tutoring, and disability-specific technology and support. In cases such as this, the colleges and uni-versities would have their own "free to the student" mentoring program, plus those services provided under a TRIO grant. This would allow the student to have access to more services.

In October, Meghan is earning C's and B's in her classes. The DSS office has provided her with the accommodations she requested. The TRIO Grant personnel mentor Meghan's academic, psychosocial, and executive function-ing about once a week and provide up to three hours a week of peer tutor-ing per subject. They have provided her with access to assistive technology available on campus. In December Meghan will complete her semester with a GPA of 2.6 and return to State U in January.

Category Three: Several colleges and universities—in addition to or in combination with the no-cost bare-bones and enhanced college mentoring programs described above—offer fee-based mentoring programs. Fee-based programs range in price from $5,000 a year—on the low end—to a whop-ping $23,000 per year—on the high end. Typically, the services provided are in accordance with the money that SWD pay. Depending on the mentoring program and money available, an institution may offer a writing center, math laboratory, an enhanced learning resource center/academic support center, sci-ence laboratory, coaching services center, social support groups, and seminars.

Staffing for the programs range from one doctoral-level person, two mas-ters-level people, and very extensive professional and peer tutors for academic and psychosocial support for twenty-five students to high-end programs offering extensive professional mentoring in ratios of one professional to four students with unlimited mentoring and tutoring available. Students already accepted at the college must apply for acceptance into the mentoring program.

Meghan is earning B's and A's in all her classes in the third month of the semester, October. She believes the $5,000 cost per semester for enhanced services is money well spent. The DSS office has provided her with the *accommodations she requested. In addition to the tutoring she receives through the TRIO Grant Program, the director and counselors in the fee-based enhanced services program at State U mentor Meghan's academic, psychosocial, and executive functioning with private sessions as often as she requests and provide her with an unlimited amount of peer tutoring. The enhanced services program's assistive technology coordinator will provide Meghan with most of the technology hardware and software she requires. Meghan will complete her semester with a GPA of 3.2 and return to State U in January.*

Category Four: To meet the mandates of the HEOA (2008), 227 colleges and universities now offer mentoring programs for students with developmental and intellectual disabilities who were not previously served on the postsecondary education level. The HEOA makes grants available to institutions of higher education to enable them to create or expand high-quality, inclusive, model comprehensive transition and postsecondary programs for students.

These innovative pilot programs offer a varied mixture of academic, psychosocial, and executive-functioning skill-mentoring services in all aspects of the institution's regular postsecondary program—including extracurricular activities. Students attending regular college courses and students attending noncredit social and life skill courses in an otherwise inclusive college environment will have special mentors plus the services available to all other students in the college. Students attending self-contained life skills programs will be mentored by the personnel overseeing them.

Tuition comes from three sources: public school districts, rehabilitation agencies, and parents. Students aged eighteen to twenty-one, whose Individualized Education Program places them in a college program, have their education paid for by their local school district. Those twenty-two and older often receive all or part of their tuition through rehabilitation agencies. The rest pay their tuition through family funds.

Oscar, a student with an intellectual disability, needs to have his intense academic, psychosocial, and executive functioning mentored. Theo, a student on the Autism Spectrum with a high IQ and excellent high school grades, will need specialized mentoring to interact with professors and classmates and control behaviors such as speaking out of turn, respecting other's boundaries, and asking too many questions. Oscar and Theo will attend an innovative pilot program at State U. This self-contained program will mentor them as needed. Oscar, nineteen years of age, will have his college paid for by his local school district. Theo, a high school graduate, will have his college paid for by his family and additional financing made available under HEOA, the Higher Education Opportunity Act.

Category Five: A few colleges exist that are for SWD only. These institutions offer small class sizes, intense personal support, an understanding of the students' disability and unique learning styles, and tools and strategies to ensure success in college.

Meghan chose to attend one of the few disability-specific colleges in the country. With a college environment designed for students with her disability, October finds her well adjusted to college life, and succeeding in the classroom. She has a successful semester and looks forward to coming back in January.

Mentoring models that are available and can be offered with any of the above-listed programs are electronic mentoring, learning communities, coaching, and assistive technology.

- **Electronic mentoring**—Pairing a skilled mentor with a disability and a mentee with a disability is ideal. Due to disability characteristics or logistics, it is often impossible to get the mentor and mentee face-to-face. Sometimes verbal communication issues can impede the process. Electronic mentoring is one possible solution. Electronic mentoring allows two or more people to communicate with each other through email, social media, Skype, and Internet communities such as chat rooms and web-based bulletin boards (Burgstahler & Crawford 2007).
- **Learning Communities**: Learning Communities (LC) are intentional, collaborative mentoring groups that work toward a common purpose. LC build valuable knowledge—collectively greater than any one individual can accrue on his or her own—accessible to everyone in the group. They can provide the context in which one sees others successfully cope and succeed. Members can provide the encouragement and constructive influence needed to enhance self-efficacy.

  LC can be credit-bearing classes where students are mentored by professors and peers to build social capital (Whitney, Langley-Turnbaugh, Lovewell, & Moeller, 2012). Social capital includes accumulated interpersonal commodities such as trust, reciprocal relationships, community membership, and other behaviors that allow individuals to act collectively (Putnam, 1995). Social capital provides resources and power allowing SWD to participate in the dominant ablest culture of the college.
- **Coaching**: According to Field, Parker, Sawilowsky, and Rolands (2013), coaching is an effective mentoring tool used to improve student learning and executive functioning skills—self-regulatory mechanisms for organizing, directing, and managing other cognitive activities, emotional responses, and overt behaviors (Gioia, Isquith, & Guy, 2001). College students with disabilities benefit from coaching services—counseling services to increase executive functioning skills—interventions adjunct to academic

and educational services usually offered by most colleges (Richman, Rademacher, & Maitland, 2014). Coaching can be offered face-to-face, through electronic communication, or a combination of both.

- **Assistive Technology**: Assistive technology hardware and software are rapidly being created or updated. They provide access and assistance to students with physical, learning, and other disabilities. Professional mentors are needed to perform an assistive technology assessment—to identify the correct technology to meet the learning, social, and executive functioning needs of mentees—and to provide ongoing mentoring in the usage of ever-evolving technology. Technology available to help mentees include the following: (1) Kurzweil 3000 (verbally reads texts and papers through the computer while highlighting words being read), (2) Classmate Reader (portable reader), (3) Inspiration Software (graphically organizes thoughts), (4) Dragon Naturally Speaking (allows mentees to dictate into a computer which types of words are spoken), (5) Scientific Notebook (software that aids in mathematical problem solving), (6) Word Q (word prediction, text-to-speech program), (7) Editor (software that helps mentees edit papers), and (8) ALEKS (a web-based program for math).

IDEAL MENTORING PROGRAM

Mentorship programs that are well resourced, planned, and designed have comprehensive implementation and evaluation plans in place before beginning. These include criteria for mentor and mentee selection and strategies to recruit and train them. Sufficient resources—time, budget, and staff—also need to be allocated (Stumbo, Lindahl-Lewis, & Blegen, 2008).

The ideal postsecondary mentoring program for SWD is a four-tiered pyramid. At the top of the pyramid in Tier One we find the leader—a professional with a terminal degree—who is an expert in academics, tutoring skills, and with knowledge of several academic areas of study at the institution. In addition, the leader has expertise in counseling and guidance, is immersed in disability life and culture, and serves as the organization and operation of the institution. Finding the correct person for this position with such a large diversified knowledge and skill set is critical. This person might be a person with a disability or a person without a disability. Of paramount importance are an activist's critical-disabilities-rights mind-set and the superior intellectual, academic knowledge, and social-emotional fund of information the person possesses.

In other words, this person has all the skills necessary to mentor all other mentors in the pyramid—college administrators, faculty, staff, and students—on the appropriate ways to mentor college SWD and will be the mentor of last resort for the students. Responsibilities will include setting up a structure for comprehensive DSS for SWD under one umbrella using available funding to meet the needs of as many students as possible.

In Tier Two we find people with extensive expertise, usually requiring an advanced degree, in one or more of the following mentoring areas: professional-level psychosocial counseling; academic subject area tutoring; management of medical, physical mobility, and dexterity issues; and financial counseling. Licensed counselors provide psychotherapy, career counseling, executive functioning coaching, and a liaison to access community resources.

Academic subject area mentors have extensive knowledge in the disciplines they tutor. In addition, they are experts in tutoring and teaching people with disabilities—as special educators—schooled in the use of UDL, in diagnosing and teaching using the mentee's strength as a resource, and with broad knowledge of available accommodations for learning and testing and how to apply them. Being able to assist mentees with the development of the executive functions needed for college success, they model communication and advocacy with the faculty and others on campus and intervene when necessary on the students' behalf.

Ideally, the umbrella of disability services houses a financial counselor with particular expertise on all sources of funding—such as funds that have been made available to students with intellectual and developmental disabilities under the HEOA and its amendments (2008)—who is able to mentor the unique needs of SWD. Last, a medically trained mentor is available to evaluate physical mobility (gross motor), occupational skills (fine motor), and provide mentees with services needed to perform in college.

Each mentee has a primary mentor—a case manager—who coordinates all aspects of the mentee's education, including DSS, the student's program of study, registration, financial aid, and interactions with faculty, college offices, and other services on campus. The primary mentor keeps mentees abreast of all services, programs, and activities available at the college. The primary mentor is the Tier Two mentor providing the most services to the mentee. For example, the primary mentor for a mentee needing extensive academic assistance is his or her academic tutor, and the primary mentor of a mentee with extensive psychosocial issues is his or her counselor. Mentees with multiple mentors choose one to be the primary mentor.

Mentors in Tier Three of the pyramid—usually with a college degree—are employees and long-term volunteers of the college. Some mentors provide mentees with academic support and tutoring, and others provide life coaching.

Peer and near-peer—an upper-level college student—mentors are found in Tier Four. These mentors provide academic support, tutoring, and social coaching to mentees in and out of the DSS center. Often accompanying mentees to social, sporting, and academic enrichment activities, they provide friendship, a social safety net, and a conduit to establish a broader social network with other students on campus.

Operationally, this four-tiered ideal mentoring program is democratic and fluid. Open communication exists between everyone involved in the process through a cyclical process of dialogue, consensus, and implementation. Mentors on each level meet with a facilitator to dialogue on successes, failures, and needed change and come to consensus. In similar fashion, mentees meet in groups of manageable size to dialogue. Then, representatives from each group gather to further the dialogue, come to greater consensus, and make a plan to implement changes to improve the program. The groups meet on a regular basis to monitor the program and make rolling improvements to maintain the ideal.

Mentors with disabilities who are part of the culture provide excellent role models for mentees. The voices these mentors can bring to their mentees and the process of dialogue, consensus, and implementation are unique and should not be overlooked. Veteran mentees with disabilities often make excellent peer and near-peer mentors. Upon acquiring higher professional degrees, they will make excellent tier three, two, and one mentors.

October of her senior year has arrived. As Meghan looked up at the robin-blue sky framing the ivy-draped buildings aflame in autumn dress, she expressed the gratitude she feels for her high school transition counselor who assisted her in finding the ideal mentoring program. When she arrived at State U, Meghan and the folks in the ideal program created a plan coordinating all programs and services on campus—updated on a rolling basis—which provided all mentoring services she needed to academically and psychosocially self-actualize. Over the years she had been mentored through electronic mentoring programs, coaching, learning communities, and in the use of assistive technology. Meghan's dreams had come true!

CONCLUSION

"Mentoring is a dynamic, reciprocal, long-term formal or informal relationship that focuses on personal and/or professional development. A mentor is a sounding board and guide. Mentors provide perspectives, resources, and ask thought-provoking questions" (Foster Heckman, Brown, & Roberts, 2007, p. 2). A quality mentor can make or break a postsecondary student with a disability.

The ideal mentor and mentee relationship should be a reciprocal one, with each learning from the other. The relationship is more casual than formal and emphasizes commitment and longevity. Time spent together includes socializing and doing nonacademic activities—not only face-to-face meetings but also using electronic media—such as text and email. One should never lose sight of the mentor and mentee relationship being a reciprocal, collaborative process (Foster Heckman, Brown, & Roberts, 2007), with mentees bringing certain motivations, actions, attitudes, and knowledge about their disability and learning to their mentors (Lunsford, 2011).

"Understanding what characteristics lead to effective mentors and mentoring programs may enhance the enrollment, retention, and matriculation rates of students with disabilities attending postsecondary institutions" (Brown, Takahashi, & Roberts, 2010, p. 110).

This chapter discussed the mentoring processes and programs that colleges and universities currently provide to SWD and closed with an ideal program to mentor college students with disabilities. The ideal postsecondary mentoring program for SWD was described as a four-tiered pyramid, providing comprehensive services to mentees with disabilities under one umbrella. Operationally democratic and fluid and involving all constituents in an ongoing process of dialogue, consensus, and implementation, the program will continually evolve to meet the mentoring needs of postsecondary students with disabilities, and others as well.

REFERENCES

Americans with Disabilities Act, 42 U.S.C. §§ 12101-213 (2006).

Brown, S. E., Takahashi, K., & Roberts, K. D. (2010). Mentoring individuals with disabilities in postsecondary education: A review of the literature. *Journal of Postsecondary Education and Disability 23* (2), 98–111.

Burgstahler, S., & Crawford, L. (2007). Managing an e-mentoring community to support students with disabilities: A case study. *AACE Journal 15* (2), 97–114.

Davis, J. (2012). Three ways to support the academic performance of students who are "neurologically atypical." *Recruitment and Retention* (September), 5–6.

Davis, L. (1997). *The disability studies reader.* New York: Routledge.

Field, S., Parker, D. R., Sawilowsky, S., & Rolands, L. (2013). Assessing the impact of ADHD coaching services on university students' learning skills, self-regulation, and well being. *Journal of Postsecondary Education and Disability 26* (1), 67–81.

Fingarette, H. (1963). *The self in transformation: Psychoanalysis, philosophy, and the life of the spirit.* New York: Basic Books.

Foster Heckman, E., Brown, S. E., & Roberts, K. D. (Fall 2007). Mentoring partnership project: Exploring mentoring practices for students with disabilities in postsecondary education. *The George Washington University HEATH Resource Center.* http://www.ist.hawaii.edu/products/.

Gil, L. (2007). Bridging the transition gap from high school to college: Preparing students with disabilities for a successful postsecondary experience. *Teaching Exceptional Children 40* (2), 12–15.

Gioia, G. A., Isquith, P. K., & Guy, S. C. (2001). Assessment of executive function in children with neurological impairments. In *Psychological and developmental assessment*. Edited by R. Simeonsson and S. Rosenthal, 317–56. New York: Guildford Press.

Higher Education Opportunities Act. P.L.110-315, 20 U.S.C. § 1001 et seq. (2008).

Individuals with Disabilities Education Improvement Act, P.L. 108-446, 118 Stat. 2647 (2004), now codified, as amended, at 20 U.S.C. § 1400-91 (2006).

Lightner, K. L., Kipps-Vaughn, D., Schulte, T., & Trice, A. D. (2012). Reasons university students with a learning disability wait to seek disability services. *Journal of Postsecondary Education and Disability 25* (2), 145–59.

Lunsford, L. G. (2011). Psychology of mentoring: The case of talented college students. *Journal of Advanced Academics 22* (3), 474–98.

Mull, C., Sitlington, P., & Alper, S. (2001). Postsecondary education for students with learning disabilities: A synthesis of the literature. *Exceptional Children 68* (1), 97–118.

National Center for Special Education Research U.S. Department Of Education (2011). The post-high school outcomes of young adults with disabilities up to 8 years after high school. Report from the national longitudinal transition study-2 (NLTS2) NCD and the Americans with Disability Act: fifteen years of progress (2005). Washington, DC: Author. http://www.ncd.gov/newsroom/publications/2005/ 15yearprogress.htm.

National Center for Education Statistics. (2003). *The condition of education 2003* (NCES 2003-067). U.S. Department of Education, Washington, DC: U.S. Government Printing Office.

National Center for Education Statistics. (2006). *The digest of education 2005* (NCES, 2006-030). U.S. Department of Education, Washington, DC: U.S. Government Printing Office.

National Center for Special Education Research, U.S. Department of Education. (2011). The post-high school outcomes of young adults with disabilities up to 8 years after high

Noddings, N. (1984). *Caring: A feminine approach to ethics and moral education.* Berkeley, CA: University of California Press.

Patrick, S., & Wessel, R. D. (2013). Faculty mentorship and transition experiences of students with disabilities. *Journal of Postsecondary Education and Disability 26* (2), 105–18.

Pingry O'Neill, L. N., Markward, M. J., & French, J. P. (2012). Predictors of graduation among college students with disabilities. *Journal of Postsecondary Education and Disability 25* (1), 21–36.

Putnam, R. D. (1995). Tuning in, turning out: The strange disappearance of social capital. *Political Science and Politics 28*, 664–83.

Rehabilitation Act, Section 504, 29 U.S.C. § 794 (2006).

Richman, E. L., Rademacher, K. N., & Maitland, T. L. (2014). Coaching and college success. *Journal of Postsecondary Education and Disability 27* (1), 43–68.

Rogers, C. (1961). *On becoming a person.* Boston: Houghton Mifflin.

Rogers, C. (1970). *Encounter groups.* New York: Harper & Row.

Ryan, S. M. (2014). An inclusive rural post secondary education program for students with intellectual disabilities. *Rural Special Education Quarterly 33* (2), 18–28.

Stumbo, N. J., Lindahl-Lewis, P., Blegen, A. R. (2008). Two mentorship case studies of high school and university students with disabilities: Milestones and lessons. *Journal of Rehabilitation 74* (3), 45–51.

Thompson-Ebanks, V. (2014). Personal factors that influence the voluntary withdrawal of undergraduates with disabilities. *Journal of Postsecondary Education and Disability 27* (2), 195–207.

Troiano, P. F., Liefeld, J. A., & Trachtenberg, J. V. (2010). Academic support and college success for postsecondary students with learning disabilities. *Journal of College Reading and Learning 40* (2), 35–44.

Whitney, J., Langley-Turnbaugh, S., Lovewell, L., Moeller, B. (2012). Building relationships, sharing resources, and opening opportunities: A STEM learning community builds social capital for students with disabilities. *Journal of Postsecondary Education and Disability 25* (2), 131–44.

Chapter 8

The Future of Mentoring

Strengthening Sustainability Through a Humanistic Approach

Samuel Thomas Martin, Phyllis F. Reggio,
and Carlos McCray

INTRODUCTION

It is important to note that mentoring is as much science as it is an art. Capable mentors are able to use theoretical constructs of mentoring to inform their interactions with mentees in complex realities. Effective mentoring programs will continue to be critical for retaining and training future educators. Although we assert that effective mentoring programs can be implemented programmatically, understanding that each dyadic (or even triadic) mentor relationship will have its own unique distinction is a key aspect of successful mentoring. The goal of this chapter is to provide a framework for educators to take a more humanistic approach to mentoring—thus strengthening the long-range sustainability of the mentoring experience.

For the past several decades, researchers have sought to quantify and qualify the quality of mentoring programs in the field of education. Borrowing from an interdisciplinary background of business, psychology, and organizational theory, the literature has clearly established a best practices model for understanding the process of mentoring in the context of the field of education. Kanter (1977) was one of the first to discuss the benefits of mentoring in a business context. Early writings by Kanter (1977) and Kram (1983) on mentoring focused on hierarchical, dyadic relationships. Dominguez and Hager (2013) suggested that the literature on mentoring in education delineated itself in three distinct perspectives: developmental-, learning-, and social-based theories. The learning theory approach to mentoring emphasizes the positive impact on the behavior of mentees. Mentors are characterized as facilitators charged with teaching mentees how to teach themselves. The social theory approach focuses on the impact that role modeling has on mentoring relationships.

The focus is on the socialization of mentees into the larger organizational culture. The field of education quickly followed; however, some scholars have suggested that mentoring programs in the field of education often lack the dexterity to serve the needs of twenty-first-century educators—both mentors and mentees (Kent, Kochan, & Green, 2013). As the field of education evolves, so should the art of mentoring, which fosters professional development and directly impacts the quality of the profession. The complexity of the intersectionality of organizational culture and individual backgrounds demands unpacking.

It has been noted that in recent years the target audience for mentoring programs has broadened. Teacher education and school leadership programs are graduating a more diverse population. In fact, there has been an increased emphasis on recruiting and retaining a more diverse group of teachers and school leaders in regard to race, gender, social class, and orientation. Thus, it only makes sense that mentoring programs evolve in response to the changing dynamics of PK–12 educators. Ultimately, increasing diversity has hastened the need for a more responsive, collaborative approach to mentoring. We offer a theoretical framework in which the needs of diverse professionals are met with an understanding of their goals, culture, and beliefs.

This chapter explores current concepts of mentoring and suggests a humanistic concept of mentoring as a model for mentoring in the twenty-first century. We present our case for the adoption of a humanistic framework as a sustainable model for formal mentoring in three ways. First, we present a theoretical framework that aligns Critical Race Pedagogy (CRP) with humanistic learning theory. Second, we examine gaps in the current discourse on the major humanistic theory of learning. Finally, we consider what humanistic mentoring looks like in the development of educational leaders and the implementation model of humanistic mentoring practices. Additionally, we provide cases from the field that illustrate the strengths of the humanistic mentoring approach. The chapter concludes with the authors sharing their vision for how using humanistic theory can positively influence the practice of mentoring in PK–12 education.

THEORETICAL FRAMEWORK

The theoretical framework envisions humanistic mentoring in alignment with CRP. We posit that humanistic mentoring, coupled with the tenets of CRP, bolster a model of collaboration. We suggest that consideration of a humanistic theory approach provides a framework for present and future educational leaders to develop effective mentoring programs that promote inquiry, retention, and sustainability that fosters a climate of collaboration and diverse perspectives.

CRP as a field of scholarship was first broached in response to the alienation and marginalization of educators and scholars of color in the traditional educational discourse (Lynn, 1999). At its core, CRP is about empowering and enabling individuals that have been systemically marginalized in formal education spaces. CRP is based on the following tenets: (a) the expansive influence of systemic racism, (b) manifestation of expressions of power by the dominant culture, (c) reflexivity, and (d) the use of CRP as an emancipatory tool (Hughes, 2011; Jennings & Lynn, 2005).

Formal education spaces, including PK–12 schools and higher educational institutions, are designed to perpetuate current power dynamics. CRP scholarship seeks to counteract this reality by offering a tool that critiques the status quo, not only illuminating what inequity looks like in the field of education but also highlighting how individuals are able to purposefully counter oppressive influence (Jennings & Lynn, 2005). Additionally, CRP provides a framework and formal language to build a constructive discourse on the various ways that social justice educators counteract the forces of systemic oppression in their professional lives.

Lynn's early work on CRP focused on explicating the specific strategies that Black social justice educators used to liberate themselves and the students they served (Lynn, 1999). Others, including Solorzano and Yosso (2000–2001), with their work on LatCrit, continued this conversation by considering how a critical race analysis is applicable for individuals outside of the African American community. CRP scholarship expands the discussion of the impact of race in education beyond static labels to emphasize the nuances of individual lived experiences, which include, but are not limited to, language, ability, and family structure (Jennings & Lynn, 2005). Critical race pedagogues seek to honor the lived experiences of the individuals they serve by acknowledging and accounting for the critical role that racialized experiences and cultural backgrounds have on these same individuals.

As previously stated, CRP scholarship has evolved in recent years to elucidate the influence of multiple layers of identity and its impact on the lived experiences of educators (Hughes, 2011). For example, as a Black male from a working-class background, I face certain challenges in my education career that relate directly to my identity. CRP is useful in that it draws out the complex and multilayered aspect of identity to consider how individuals manage identities that invoke both positive and negative components of privilege. Race and gender identity have physical manifestations; however, other aspects of identity including orientation and social class are not readily seen by others yet have a profound impact on the lives of educators and those they educate. Furthermore, CRP scholars have sought ways to apply CRP as an emancipatory tool for practitioners in the field.

In our discussion of mentoring, we find that CRP is helpful in two distinct ways. First, it is helpful in its open and honest critique of the oppressive inclinations inherent in the structure of the American education system. Second, it is helpful in its acknowledgment of the intersectionality of identity and the complexities of its impact on the lived experiences of individuals. Identities are not developed in a vacuum, and effective mentors recognize that societal factors including racism, sexism, and classism directly influence how individuals make meaning of their experiences in PK–12 formal education spaces.

The literature on mentoring focuses heavily on the process yet marginalizes the influence that context has on the mentoring process. Systemic and contextual factors that impact the mentoring process have been undertheorized in the literature. For example, Patton (2009) found a paucity of literature on the mentoring among women in general and among African American women. Critical theories, such as CRP, focus on the critiquing of and countering established systems of power including racism, classism, and sexism. The intersectionality of identity demands that mentors are able to deftly provide mentoring that is contextually relevant to potential mentees. In this regard, humanistic mentoring offers a framework that supports self-actualization and critical consciousness. Each of these aspects of this model requires mentors and mentees to be fully invested in the mentoring process. In essence, the humanistic approach is about establishing the individuals at the center of the mentoring process.

HUMANISTIC THEORY OF LEARNING

Learning theories play an important role in understanding how learning occurs. The humanistic theory of learning involves the concept of learning through watching the behavior of others and what results from that behavior. However, learning does not have to involve a behavior change. Learning comes about as a result of observation (Barrett, 2006). Researchers in the humanistic tradition like Ryan and Frederick (1997) postulate that actualization of potentialities and fulfillment of basic needs lead to a high level of happiness and satisfaction, enthusiasm, and vitality. As new need fulfillment experiences are integrated into the general image that people hold concerning themselves and others, they become personal resources that help people cope with challenges and allow them to support and nurture others. Hence, the humanistic approach offers the opportunity for personal growth and empathy.

The conception of mentoring that emphasizes a concern for the mentee as a person—called humanistic mentoring—is anchored in humanistic psychology, arising out of the work of Maslow (1954), Rogers (1961), and Noddings (1992). Rogers's (1961) "person-centered approach," for example, advocates for the professional therapist to recognize "the individual has within himself or herself vast resources for self-understanding" (p. 98), and that given the proper climate for change, the individual can embrace their positive qualities in a realistic way and begin to grow.

Cain's (2001) model is congruent with this framework emphasizing the humanistic belief that people possess the rights and ability to generate their own goals, both personally and professionally, and actively to develop achievable plans to meet their self-constructed goals. Humanstic mentors, like critical race pedagogues, co-construct relationships with mentees that are culturally salient and mutually beneficial. Placing the individual at the center of the mentoring process emphasizes the agency of mentees.

Effective mentoring considers not only the individual factors such as skill development but also the effect that the social context the individual negotiates has on the mentoring process. Accordingly, humanistic mentoring emphasizes the development of agency. Applied to an educational setting, we envision humanistic mentoring as a model, which carefully considers the mentee's professional *and* personal growth, and demonstrates an understanding and appreciation of a mentee's life, culture, and goals, both inside and outside of the institution.

Bain (2004) (see Reddick article) found that professors investing in an understanding of students' lives, goals, and cultures garnered higher gains in student achievement. Varney's (2009) exploration of humanistic mentoring in the educational realm suggests traditional mentoring models have fallen short with regard to teacher retention. Perhaps the same holds true for the high rate of principal and superintendent turnover (Norton, 2001; Cooper, Fusarelli, & Carella, 2000), or the low representation of diverse populations in top-line educational leadership positions.

Our aim is to suggest a mentoring model that can equip the mentee with sustainable habits that foster ongoing professional growth and encourages the mentee to shape beliefs and stretch beyond the mastery of tasks—while empowering mentees with self-direction. We seek to broaden the conversation in which individualized needs of mentees are thoughtfully considered.

GAPS IN CURRENT DISCOURSE

The shortcomings of the current discourse in mentoring are twofold—gaps in quality and gaps in the quantity of quality. Darwin (2000, see Patton article) stated, "Traditionally, the mentoring relationship has been framed in a language of paternalism and dependence and stems from a power-depended, hierarchical relationship, aimed at maintaining the status quo" (p. 197). Hargreaves and Fullan (2000) noted that the current discourse on mentoring in education needed to address ways in which the mentoring process can become more collaborative, as well as culturally and contextually relevant. This suggestion is not a necessarily a new concept; scholars and practitioners have noted that the most effective mentoring programs are authentic and applicable (Kent et al., 2013; Zellers, Howard, & Barcic, 2008).

Kram (1985) described good mentoring as a delicate dance requiring mentors to use soft skills such as empathy or listening while also focusing on building the capacity of mentees in hard skill areas such as subject content and procedural-based information. All stakeholders understand the importance of mentoring programs that engage both novice and experienced educators. The challenge is developing an approach that is structured enough to provide guidance yet malleable enough to allow for individualized implementation with the capacity to sustain long-term use.

Dominguez and Hager (2013) categorized the literature on mentoring into three distinct approaches: developmental, learning, and social. The developmental approach describes much of the early literature on mentoring, which viewed the process as a journey through rigid stages and plateaus and does not adequately address practical issues such as diversity. Learning-based mentoring approaches focus on mentors helping mentees develop the specialized skills and knowledge necessary as the mentor assumes the role of a coach/facilitator (Dominguez & Hager, 2013). The social approach to mentorship recognizes that mentoring is a dynamic process that involves significant engagement from both mentors and mentees.

Additionally, social-based approaches suggest that mentoring does not have to be dyadic. Individuals are not limited to having one mentor that fulfills all their needs. Mentees are just as responsible as mentors are for the success of the mentoring relationship. That being said, the onus is on current leaders in the field to ensure that future professionals are able to get their mentoring needs met in a manner that is purposeful and practical and equips the mentee with long-term tools for success. In this regard, we offer the humanistic theory of learning as a concept for sustaining a collaborative and effective mentoring process. Next, we seek to illustrate the concept of humanistic mentoring by discussing the connection of theory to practice, the teaching of humanistic mentoring, and its implementation.

LINKING THEORY AND PRACTICE: WHAT DOES IT LOOK LIKE?

Varney (2009) states: "The overarching goal of Humanistic Mentoring is to empower a mentee's present and future educational and professional development through a trusting, caring relationship. The role of the professor, supervisor, or fellow teacher implementing humanistic mentoring is best characterized by an attitude of genuine caring for the person within the developing professional" (p. 219). Humanistic mentoring moves from task oriented to relationship oriented.

Given the changing nature of all roles in the profession, teachers, principals, and superintendents face daunting pressures such as meeting achievement targets, understanding the needs of communities, and sometimes finding themselves merely trying to survive in the given role. Good mentors can facilitate strategic planning and assist the mentee with tools and coaching supports, resulting in a well-run classroom or school. But what of the educator's personal challenges that can undermine successful outcomes for the mentee, such as balancing home and work life, time management, and job satisfaction or their belief systems, and backgrounds that may bring challenges to the position?

These personal qualities and issues, when left unnoticed, may inhibit the mentee's support and thus limit their learning to technical skills. Hall (2008) advocates that building self-reflection skills is paramount to effectuating lasting support for the protégé. Mentoring from a humanistic approach encourages the mentee to share these personal issues with the mentor. The mentor, within this relationship, serves as a caring listener and thinking partner willing to similarly offer their own personal perspectives and experiences and work through situations by tapping into interpersonal relationships, fostering independence, and engaging as a colleague walking the path together.

The humanistic approach to mentoring seeks to shape the mentee's facility in self-reflection. This reflective practice according to Pack (2009) (see Colon article) requires the presence of trust, mutuality, and timely feedback on the part of the mentor. Thus, it is incumbent upon the mentor to facilitate a climate of mutual trust and respect at the onset of the process—no easy task. This begs the question, "How can we train mentors in humanism?" Thus, we explore several approaches to the facilitation of humanistic mentoring.

TEACHING HUMANISM

Although educational leaders have made progress in increasing the availability of mentoring programs in order for mentoring programs to increase their effectiveness, they need to be more responsive to the needs of mentees (Dominguez & Hager, 2013; Norman & Ganser, 2004). Strategies such as listening, planning, and collaborating become essential tools for the humanistic mentor to use.

The first and foremost characteristic of the humanistic approach that mentors must exhibit is the ability to listen. Listening with purpose and intention is a learned skill that takes time to master. Historically, mentoring relationships have been viewed as hierarchal or top down in nature. The lived experiences and perspective that mentees offer do not compete, nor should they. Humanistic mentors advocate for the acknowledgment and appreciation of what mentees bring into the relationship. They gain perspective into the lives of the mentees, starting with mentors providing their mentees with opportunities to share their perspective on their goals, strengths, and challenges. Listening reinforces the value for mentees and assures them that the focus on the mentoring relationship will be relevant to mentees.

Second, the focus of mentoring should be on the development of the mentee, not on the end goal. Although end goals are important, a humanistic approach challenges mentors to focus more on the individual and their process. When the end goal supersedes human development, the mentoring practices become less effective, regardless of how important the milestone. Whether it is the designation of a highly effective teacher, completing a dissertation, or earning tenure, the focus of humanistic mentoring is always on the improvement of the mentee. Without a clear focus, mentoring interactions can become rote and habitualized. A humanistic mentoring approach centers the focus of mentoring on the development of the individual. It is here that potential roadblocks to development may be discovered and explored, thus enabling progress toward attaining the goal.

It is also important for mentors to embrace the reality that knowledge is context driven and often experiential in nature. Humanistic mentoring recognizes that mentoring has value for experiences inside *and* outside the professional environment, and it encourages both mentors and mentees to make such connections. Effective mentors are flexible in their expectations and allow mentees to assume ownership over the mentoring process. For example, a student teaching intern, working with a supervising host teacher, may want to receive input from their mentor on career planning, in addition to receiving feedback on her pedagogical approach. In keeping with a humanistic approach, the mentor would be a willing listener and support the discussion, realizing it has meaning to the mentee.

Finally, humanistic mentors can increase the agency and autonomy of mentees by allowing them to take the lead in the mentoring relationship, oftentimes throughout the process. This strategy can be initiated by mentees' asking questions of mentors. We've provided a list of questions that mentors might ask their mentees, as follows:

1. What specific areas that you would like to focus on in our mentoring relationship?
2. What are your goals for this mentoring relationship?
3. What are your professional goals?

4. What are your personal goals?
5. How can I assist you in achieving those goals?

This list is not exhaustive. Rather, these questions can and should be modified to reflect the specificity of one's particular mentoring situation and guide early interactions between mentors and mentees.

Application by the mentor on listening, first putting a focus on the development of the mentee, and then the strategic alignment of goals equips the humanistic mentor in building the person-centered relationship. We explore this relationship with an example from current practice and a discussion of implications.

IMPLEMENTATION OF HUMANISTIC MENTORING PRACTICES

Humanistic mentoring is about relationship building. Effective mentors are sincere and forthright with mentees. They value the expertise that mentees bring into the mentoring relationship. Humanistic mentors recognize that mentees are novice professionals; yet nonetheless, they are professionals and are worthy contributors to the relationship. Humanistic mentors resist notions of paternalism (and maternalism), which harken back to tenets of CRP garnering respect for the mentee's value system and personal beliefs. Michael, a veteran principal and mentor in New York, captured this idea. He connected with his mentee's concerns and collaborated with him on a solution that met his mentee's needs. He describes his experience here:

> I was assigned as a mentor to a new principal of a phase-in school. My mentee was in a situation where he had to encourage parents to enroll their children, but there was no awareness on the part of the community about the new phase-in school. No one knew about it or what it would offer the kids. The parents and the community were discouraged because the prior school, which was phased out, had a poor reputation and this made my mentee very anxious about how to approach this community.

The parents felt left out of the process. So did the community. It was a very poor, urban area and the school would be serving many Title I students so there was a lot of need for buy-in. He was really at a loss because he also did not know the community well. At first we talked about his ideas for the school theme, what kind of vision he had, and also about the district's requirements. This gave him a chance to bounce ideas back and forth. I asked him about his concerns and what he felt I could do to help him in the best way possible. He talked about his concerns in not knowing the community and his beliefs that without community buy-in, the school would not have a good chance at succeeding.

I suggested we identify community leaders that we would contact together and begin to set up meetings for the purpose of introductions and collaboration on the needs of the community. Once he saw that people were accepting the invitations, he was very relieved and early on he was able to connect with key members of the community. By the end of the first year, he was running monthly advisory board sessions with his community leaders and families.

Michael allowed his mentee to take the lead. He gave him the autonomy needed to express his concerns and needs while carefully tending to the mentee's belief system of building community with a sense of urgency. Rather than prescribe skills, Michael worked from the mentee's needs, gave him voice, and quickly responded with a game plan.

IMPLICATIONS AND CONCLUSIONS

The malleability of the humanistic approach to mentoring provides it with long-range relevance and the versatility to be adopted in both PK–12 and higher education settings and fosters a model of collaboration that others can follow. Educational leaders are responsible for building the capacity of future generations, and this chapter provides a framework for beginning that conversation. Effective mentoring is critical to developing sustainable excellence among educators in PK–12 education. There is a need for scholars to continue to theorize the mentoring process as well as to conduct critical examinations of how mentoring programs can be used to promote equity and agency for both mentors and mentees. Through our exploration of humanistic mentoring intersecting with CRP, we suggest several recommendations with regard to future research and professional practice.

1. Conduct research that studies long-range effects of humanistic mentoring, including its influence on new employees' retention, leadership development, and professional climate.
2. Conduct research that explores the intersectionality of multiple aspects of identity including age, race, and gender and how these factors impact mentor-mentee relationships.
3. Enlist and formally train retired educators for mentoring positions, applying a humanistic approach.

Retirees bring a wealth of experience and have the ability to provide time on a regular basis to work with mentees. Retired educators also understand the challenges of the position yet are no longer bound by mandates and district policy. Given their autonomy, they may be more inclined to offer a broadened view of solutions and situations. Likewise, this is another area for future research.

REFERENCES

Bain, K. (2004). *What the best college teachers do.* Cambridge, MA: Harvard University Press.

Barrett, L. F. (2006). Solving the emotion paradox: Categorization and the experience of emotion. *Personality and Social Psychology Review*, 10, 20–46.

Cain, D. J. (2001). Defining characteristics, history, and evolution of humanistic psychotherapies. In *Humanistic psychotherapies: Handbook of research practice*, 3–54. Edited by D. J. Cain & J. Seeman. Washington, DC: American Psychological Association.

Cooper, B. S., Fusarelli, L., & Carella, V. (2000). *Career crisis in the superintendency? The results of a national survey.* Arlington, VA: American Association of School Administrators.

Darwin, A. (2000). Critical reflections on mentoring in work settings. *Adult Education Quarterly 50* (3), 197–211.

Dominguez, N., & Hager, M. (2013). Mentoring frameworks: Synthesis and critique. *International Journal of Mentoring and Coaching in Education 2* (3), 171–88. doi:10.1108/IJMCE-03-2013-0014.

Ryan, R. M. & Frederick, C. (1997). On energy, personality, and health: Subjective vitality as a dynamic reflection of well-being. *Journal of Personality 65*, 529–65, doi: 10.1111/j.1467-6494.1997.tb00326.x.

Hall, P. (2008). Building bridges: Strengthening the principal induction process through intentional mentoring. *Phi Delta Kappan 89* (6), 449–52.

Hargreaves, A., & Fullan, M. (2000). Mentoring in the new millennium. *Theory into Practice 39* (5), 50–56.

Hughes, S. (2011). Justice for all or justice for just us? Toward a critical race pedagogy of hope through *Brown* in urban education. *Urban Education 46* (1), 99–110.

Jennings, M. E., & Lynn, M. (2005). The house that race built: Critical race pedagogy, African American education, and the reconceptualization of a critical race pedagogy. *Educational Foundations 19* (3), 15–32.

Kanter, R. M. (1977). *Men and women of the corporation.* New York: Basic Books.

Kent, A. M., Kochan, F., & Green, A. M. (2013). Cultural influences on mentoring programs and relationships: A critical review of research. *International Journal of Mentoring and Coaching in Education 2* (3), 204–17. doi:10.1108/IJMCE-08-2013-0047.

Kram, K. E. (1983). Phases of the mentor relationship. *Academy of Management Journal 6*, 608–25.

Kram, K. E. (1985). *Mentoring at work: Developmental relationships in organizational life.* Glenview, IL: Scott, Foresman.

122   *Samuel Thomas Martin, Phyllis F. Reggio, and Carlos McCray*

Lynn, M. (1999). Toward a critical race pedagogy. A research note. *Urban Education 33* (5), 606–26. doi: 10.1177/0042085999335004.

Lynn, M., Jennings, M. E., & Hughes, S. (2013). Critical race pedagogy 2.0: Lessons from Derrick Bell. *Race Ethnicity and Education 16* (4), 603–28. doi:10.1080/13613324.2013.817776.

Maslow, A. H. (1954). *Motivation and personality.* New York: Harper.

Nodding, N. (1992). *The challenge to care in schools: An alternative approach to education.* New York: Teachers College Press.

Norman, D. M., & Ganser, T. (2004). A humanistic approach to new teacher mentoring: A counseling perspective. *Journal of Humanistic Counseling, Education and Development, 43* (2), 129–40. doi:10.1002/j.2164-490X.2004.tb00013.x.

Norton, M. S. (2001). *The school superintendency in Arizona: A research study.* Tempe, AZ: Arizona State University.

Pack, M. (2009). Clinical supervision: An interdisciplinary review of literature with implications for reflective practice in social work. *Reflective Practice 10*, 657–68.

Patton, L. (2009). My sister's keeper: A qualitative examination of mentoring experiences among African American women in graduate and professional schools. *Journal of Higher Education 80* (5) (September/October), 510–37.

Rogers, C. R. (1961). *On becoming a person.* Boston: Houghton Mifflin.

Ryan, R. M. & Frederick, C. (1997). On energy, personality, and health: Subjective vitality as a dynamic reflection of well-being. *Journal of Personality*, 65, 529–65, doi: 10.1111/j.1467-6494.1997.tb00326.x.

Solorzano, D. G. & Yosso, T. J. (2001). From racial stereotyping and deficit discourse toward a critical race theory in teacher education. *Multicultural Education*, 9, 2–8.

Varney, J. (2009). Humanistic mentoring: Nurturing the person within. *Kappa Delta Kappa Record* (Spring), 127–31.

Zellers, D. F., Howard, V. M., & Barcic, M. A. (2008). Faculty mentoring programs: Envisioning rather than reinventing the wheel. *Review of Educational Research 78* (3), 552–88. doi:10.3102/0034654308320966.

Index

About the Editors and Contributors

Dr. Dagoberto Artiles is currently a school administrator in the Jericho Union Free School District in Nassau, New York, and has been employed at this institution since 2013. Dr. Artiles's administrative responsibilities include assisting in the development of effective teaching and learning environments, creating connections with the community, and innovating existing programs.

Dr. Tyrone Bynoe is currently an associate professor of education at the University of the Cumberlands in Williamsburg, Kentucky, and has been employed at this institution since 2004. Dr. Bynoe's instructional responsibilities are comprised of teaching courses in Educational Leadership with interests in school finance, effective schools, teacher quality, organizational behavior, public school supervision, educational history, and computer applications.

Sharon Conley, PhD, is a professor of education in the Gevirtz Graduate School of Education at the University of California, Santa Barbara. She is the editor, with Bruce S. Cooper, of *Moving from Teacher Isolation to Collaboration: Enhancing Professionalism and School Quality* and *Keeping and Improving Today's School Leaders: Retaining and Sustaining the Best.*

Bruce S. Cooper, PhD, is an emeritus professor of Education Leadership at Fordham University's Graduate School of Education in New York City, where he taught for thirty-four years. He has published forty books, including those on school policy (*Better Policies, Better Schools* with Vance Randall and Lance Fusarelli); politics (*Handbook of Education Politics and Policy* coedited with James Cibulka and Lance Fusarelli); and private education (*Home Schooling in Full View*).

Terrence E. Deal, PhD, is an internationally renowned speaker and writer specializing in organizations and leadership coming both from his time as a teacher, principal, and administrator and from his research as a professor. He previously held professorships at Stanford, Harvard, Vanderbilt, and University of Southern California (USC) and resides in San Luis Obispo, California.

Dr. Samuel Martin holds a doctorate in Educational Leadership, a Master of Education in School Counseling, and a Bachelor of Science in Middle School Education, each from the University of Missouri–Columbia. His research interest focuses on the impact of race, class, and gender on school culture and academic achievement. Samuel is currently employed as a professional school counselor with Columbia Public Schools in Columbia, Missouri.

Dr. Carlos R. McCray is division chair and associate professor in Educational Leadership, Administration, and Policy Division at Fordham University Graduate School of Education, New York. He is the coauthor of the books *Cultural Collision and Collusion: Reflections on Hip-Hop Culture, Values, and Schools*; *and School Leadership in a Diverse Society: Helping Schools Prepare All Students for Success.* Professor McCray has worked with school leaders and educators in the metropolitan areas of Atlanta, New York, and London.

Dr. Laverne C. Nimmons is currently a New York City Department of Education (NYCDOE) and Council of Supervisors and Administrators/Supervisory Support program intervener/mentor. Dr. Nimmons has worked with the NYCDOE for thirty-two years as a principal of a National Blue Ribbon School of Excellence, an assistant principal, and a teacher.

Donna Redman, EdD, is an assistant professor of education in the College of Education and Organizational Leadership at the University of La Verne in La Verne, California. She currently teaches a variety of courses in the undergraduate Educational Studies program in the Department of Education and Teacher Development, where she leads the Educational Studies program as chairperson.

Phyllis Reggio, EdD, is a supervisory support specialist at the Center for Educational Innovation, a private association in New York City that provides public school principals with individualized leadership support. Prior to this, she served as a local superintendent, principal, and assistant principal.

Dr. Reggio's research interest lies in all aspects of women in educational leadership.

Dr. Carol Strax is an associate professor at Dominican College in Orangeburg, New York, where she teaches inclusive and special education classes. A qualitative researcher, her interests include the politics of special education, the use of service dogs with people with disabilities, and children's literature.

Dr. Marshall Strax, an advocate for people with disabilities, is a professor at the College of Saint Elizabeth in Morristown, New Jersey. His interests include the intersection of disability studies and special education, the politics of special education, and life in higher education and disabilities.

Chun Zhang, PhD, is a full professor at the Division of Curriculum and Teaching, Graduate School of Education, Fordham University. Her research focuses on early prevention and intervention of developmental delays and disabilities for young children, from birth to age eight, family-professional partnerships and collaboration, and teacher training and effectiveness.